PERSON TO PERSON

Making Connections With Others and Yourself

*For Bea ~
to the joys
of connecting!
Elizabeth Jeffries*

ELIZABETH JEFFRIES

The Leadership Press

ISBN 0-9627459-1-X
Printed in U.S.A.

**Attention corporations, sales groups, colleges,
universities and other organizations:**
This book may be purchased at bulk discount
rates for use in educational programs, or as
premiums in sales promotions or fund raising
campaigns. Abridged versions, excerpts, or other
modified versions may be arranged through the
publisher. For details contact The Leadership
Press, P.O. Box 24475, Louisville, Kentucky
40224, (502) 339-1600 or 800-285-8500.

Dedication

In loving memory of Vincent Coors
who helped me make my own inner connection.

Acknowledgements

Nothing of merit has ever been accomplished alone, and so it is with this book. Several significant people in my life have helped me to grow, take risks and supported my belief that one person can indeed make a difference.

My gratitude goes to my family for always loving me unconditionally, to Bill Edwards who believed in me at a time when I saw very little to believe in, and to my colleagues in the National Speakers Association who have so generously shared their time and knowledge over the past years.

My deepest appreciation goes to Mary Rivard, my friend and associate, for the countless hours she spent in editing this book and coaching me about my speaking career. Her understanding, support and dedication to my mission have enabled me to continuously reach new heights of growth.

Perhaps the greatest debt, though, is owed to all those women and men who have ever been in my audience. They were the ones who inspired and encouraged me to write this book. But most importantly, they affirmed and helped deepen my spiritual connection with God.

—Elizabeth Nardi Jeffries

"I was abandoned to a thousand thoughts, and for many days, had attempted mightily to discover myself and what was good for me, and what evil to avoid, when suddenly — was it myself or was it another, I do not know, and that was precisely what I ardently sought to know. Anyway, it was said to me, 'If you find what you seek, what will you do with it? Who will you entrust it to before you die?'

"I answered, 'I will keep it in my memory.'

"'But can your memory keep everything your mind has perceived? Indeed, it cannot. You must write, then...ask for strength so that you may find what you seek: then write it down, so that this child-bearing of your heart may quicken it and make it strong. Write only the results, and spare the words. Think not of the many that may read these pages, a few will understand.'"

St. Augustine
(Opening Lines of "The Soliloquy")

Contents

PROLOGUE viii

Section I: Connecting With Yourself

Chapter One

The Power Connection 3

Chapter Two

Stop the World, I Want to Get On 17

Chapter Three

Take Full Responsibility for Your Own Life 35

Chapter Four

Accept Yourself As You Are, and Go from There... 53

Chapter Five

Believe in Yourself 69

Chapter Six

Target Your Life 85

Section II: Balance Your Life

Chapter Seven

    Pinpointing Stress in Your Life 109

Chapter Eight

    Understanding How Stress Affects You 125

Chapter Nine

    Self-Management Techniques for Balancing 137

Chapter Ten

    It's About Time 155

Section III: The Soul of Leadership

Chapter Eleven

    Your Leading Edge 174

Chapter Twelve

    Mastering Effective Communication 185

Epilog 180

E L I Z A B E T H   J E F F R I E S

$\mathcal{P}$rologue

Something dramatic began to happen that day in 1982, but I had no way of knowing how radically it would change my life, my career, and all my relationships.

A medical society group had booked me because I was a professional speaker, a management consultant, and had a strong background in the health services field.

My speech had been carefully researched, written out, and rehearsed. Ever since I started in this business, I studied the techniques of the best professional speakers in the country and tried diligently to follow their guidance.

When you're only five feet tall, hiding behind a lectern feels pretty safe. And that's exactly what I was doing in all my speeches — playing it safe.

But it wasn't real; it wasn't me. I'd listen to the recordings of my speeches and ask, "Who is this person speaking?"

The expressions of people in that large audience seemed to be pleading, "Please! Don't play games with us! Tell us who you really are! It'll help us discover who we are!"

Almost before I realized what was happening, I grabbed my notes and the mic, and started walking right out into the audience.

"I don't know why I'm speaking from behind there," I said as I stepped from behind the lectern. "I want to come out here where I can look you in the eye and be close to you!"

Suddenly, I felt as if I were a butterfly breaking out of a cocoon and flexing its wings. Something powerful was going on inside me. The crowd saw it happening, and soon people were breaking out of cocoons all over that auditorium. Together, we made some great discoveries that day.

"Elizabeth, we want you to come back next year," one of the group's leaders said to me later, "because you're real! The stories you tell, the way you project yourself...you're not phony! You've lived the things you're talking about...you've struggled with the issues you invite us to struggle with.... You make it less threatening for us to deal with the things we fear most."

A light flashed on inside me! I had gotten precisely the results I'd wanted, but in a totally unexpected way.

It had not been my professional skills as a speaker that had produced the results, although professional skills are of utmost importance. Nor had my carefully chosen words and ideas (as important as they are) made the difference. Even the physical act of walking out into the audience could not have produced such a dramatic impact.

What had transformed that speech into in-depth communication was that I had made a connection with the people by getting real.

What had transformed that speech into in-depth communication was that I had made a connection with the people by getting real. I had pulled off my mask and given them the real Elizabeth Jeffries and, much to my surprise and delight, that's exactly what they wanted from me all along.

A union, a connection is what happens when the reality in you touches the reality in others, and together you move on to a new reality. You're changed, they're changed, and the relationship between you is forever altered.

That experience opened up a whole new way of thinking and acting for me. It showed me I have a gift and a responsibility to use it. By allowing people to share in my struggles with life's tough challenges, I could give them the hope, the faith, and the courage to keep going — no matter how tough it gets. By loving people enough to get vulnerable with them, I could set them free to risk loving and receiving love.

I began to understand that nothing produces response as effectively as responsiveness. And that is what this whole book is about:

- Connecting with yourself by getting real.

- Connecting with others by getting real.

- Getting more positive outcomes in all your personal and professional relationships.

You won't be reading empty theories about living and working with people. I'm not an expert with all the answers.

Instead, I'll share with you my search, my struggles, victories, and some ideas and techniques I've found very useful along the way. Hopefully, you'll be able to identify with some of my experiences and feelings. Perhaps they'll even enable you to make some exciting discoveries about your own life.

It's scary business, this inviting you into my thoughts and feelings. As I send this book out to you, I can

E L I Z A B E T H   J E F F R I E S

connect in a new way with the timid soul who said:
"I'm afraid to tell you who I am,
because, if I tell you who I am,
you may not like who I am,
and it's all that I have."[1]

Yet there's a certain quiet inner confidence I feel about it all, a confidence born of many experiences in reaching out to literally thousands of people and seeing countless responses which seem to say, "Yes! I see what you mean!" and "Me too, Elizabeth."

Also, there's the confidence which comes from knowing these ideas and insights really work because I've proved them in my own life, and I've watched as they've worked for countless others. I believe they'll work for you.

You may also find it a little scary because I'm going to invite you to ask some hard questions about your own personal and professional life. But you'll also find plenty of opportunities to search for ways you can improve the quality of all your relationships and boost your productivity by sharing yourself more fully with those you live and work with every day.

I hope you'll exercise the courage to break out of your cocoon and flex your wings in a new way. You might discover that you're more than a butterfly. You may even begin to feel like an eagle. One thing I know for sure: you'll love the impact inner connecting makes on you, and on all your personal and professional relationships!

---

1.   Powell, John S.J., why am i afraid to tell you who i am?, Copyright © 1969 by
     Argus Communications, Chicago.supported my belief that one person can
     indeed make a difference.

E L I Z A B E T H   J E F F R I E S

SECTION I

Connecting With Yourself

You can't teach a person anything; you can only help him discover it within himself.

—Galileo

One

The Power Connection

Objectives

1. To see how getting real enables you to connect with yourself and others in a powerful way.

2. To understand what it means to get real with yourself and others.

3. To search out why getting real with yourself and others gets such powerful results.

*Getting Real...doesn't happen all at once," said
the Skin Horse. "You become. It takes a long time.
That's why it doesn't happen to people who break
easily or have sharp edges, or have to be carefully
kept.*

— Margery Williams
The Velveteen Rabbit

Inner Connecting: The Personal Touch

You walk down a busy street, jostling your way through the crowd. You're in a hurry; you've got places to go; you've got things on your mind. It's as if all those people are not there.

Suddenly, among that mass of people, you see a familiar face! It's someone you know very well; someone you care very much about.

Quickly, you begin waving your arms, shouting, trying to attract the person's attention. But you're also just another face in the crowd. The person doesn't even notice you.

As you draw closer, you begin shouting the person's name. You see them break stride and begin searching through the crowd for you. When your eyes meet, you smile, greet each other, and begin walking along together. It's as if you're the only two people on that street.

What's happened? You've:
• seen a familiar face;
• made yourself known;
• expressed the affection you feel.

The other person has:
• heard a familiar voice;
• heard a familiar name;
• seen a familiar face.

You've made the personal connection — the power connection.

That's what inner connecting is all about. It is:
- knowing the reality within yourself.
- revealing your inner reality to others.
- knowing and caring what matters to them.
- coming *from the inside out*.

It all starts with getting real: getting real with yourself and getting real with others.

And it's powerful stuff, this inner connecting! It can
transform dull relationships into dynamite, enable you
to communicate more effectively, and help you to get
things moving in every area of your life.

What does it mean to get real?

Certainly it means more than the pseudo-honesty so
many hide behind to justify airing all their gripes to
and about people. To be sure, there's more involved
than the "sensitivity training" sessions which once
gave thousands of people a good excuse to yell at each
other.

The dictionary uses words like "genuine, " actual,
and "true" to define real.

I've found getting real to be a little like peeling off
the layers of an onion. Each layer you peel away
reveals another layer, until you finally come to the
center. There, you find a tiny seed which has fantastic
possibilities. Here are some clues I've found to be
useful.

Getting Real is Living "Without Wax"

Our word "sincere" comes from combining the two
Latin words "sine" and "cera", and literally means
"without wax."

It's a term which grew out of the ancient Roman practice of pawning off flawed statues, with their flaws carefully concealed by wax. It was a criminal practice which eventually carried a death penalty. Thus, Roman citizens knew they could count on getting a genuine statue wherever they saw the "sine cera" sign.

All of us have flaws, and many of us have become pretty good at hiding them. In fact, sometimes we are so good at it we even fool ourselves.

Getting real means accepting the fact that we're not perfect and facing up to our flaws.

Getting real means accepting the fact that we're not perfect and facing up to our flaws. It's something most of us find easy to pay lip service to but hard to really do.

Getting Real Is Recognizing True Value

One reason it's so hard to accept and deal with our flaws is that most of us have little understanding of just how valuable we are as human beings created in the image of God.

Unfortunately, we live in a culture which values people according to what they do, not what they are. So it is not unusual for an athlete to make 10 times the salary of a school teacher. Of course, where money is the primary method of keeping score, the value of people can become grossly distorted.

Getting real means pushing through those distortions to discover our own true value and the true value of other human beings. It's learning to value people and use things - not vice versa.

ELIZABETH   JEFFRIES

Getting Real Is Coming to Grips with People Potential

Most of us have a very limited view of our potential as capable individuals. We may get glimpses of it from time to time when we are surprised at something extraordinary we've accomplished. But even those fleeting glimpses tend to get lost in the "dailiness" of life.

Likewise, we often fail to see the full potential of people who surround us. Maybe it's our preoccupation with what we want others to do which clouds our vision of what they can become.

Whatever it is that limits our reverence for the greatness which is within us and all around us, it often keeps us from receiving and giving the best life has to offer.

Getting real means awakening the sleeping giant within us, and giving all the people who share our lives a glimpse of the potential we see in them.

Getting Real Is Becoming Your Own Person

Professor Marshall McCluhan is right, you know. We are so massaged by the media that the average person's goal seems to be to become an average person.

There's a cookie-cutter sameness mentality running rampant in our society. We've got designer jeans, status symbol cars, and modular furniture. There's even a decreed look for the "punkers," who are protesting all the lack of individuality.

Getting real is cutting through all the labels to connect with the unique person each of us is. It's finding our own gifts and taking the risk to offer them to the world around us.

Getting Real Is Allowing Others To Be Themselves

When we meet someone whose views and actions are vastly different from ours, many of us feel a strong urge to either become like them or force them to become like us. It's a strange quirk of human nature since most of us are attracted to, or at least complemented by, opposites.

Perhaps this overpowering urge to change people stems from our uncertainties about our own identity. It seems the less secure we are in our own personhood, the more we feel a need to control everybody around us.

Getting real is giving people the freedom to be themselves. But it's more than the empty "live and let live" credo espoused by many. It involves receiving each person's unique gifts, celebrating their individuality, and helping them to become all they were created to be.

In later chapters, we'll focus on how to discover a new level of being real with yourself and others. Right now, let's explore a big question.

Why Is Getting Real So Powerful?

There's one thing none of us can do. We can't follow the movements of our own eyes, even in a mirror. At the slightest movement of our eyes, our gaze shifts to a new focal pint. Thus, this most telling window through which we might glimpse our own inner lives is closed to us.

In a way, that interesting bit of trivia symbolizes jut how hard it is to really get to know our true selves. Some of us spend years searching for clues as to who we are, why we feel as we do, and why we do many of the things we do.

Let's face it. We all have a deep need to be loved, to be affirmed, to matter to others. Because we are lonely and afraid, we reach out to those around us.

> *We all have a deep need to be loved, to be affirmed, to matter to others.*

If others draw back from us because of their own hang-ups, we feel rejected, hurt, crushed. It confirms our deepest fears about ourselves.

But when someone cares enough to become real with us, it gives us a new freedom to reach in and touch ourselves. Their vulnerability strips away our defensiveness and enables us to ask those unaskable questions. Their honesty affirms our value as persons and gives us the courage to risk revealing our true selves.

This miraculous process of dialogue with another human being is so liberating it radically alters our perceptions of ourselves and our feelings about others.

Of course, the kind of openness I'm talking about goes far beyond the "open door policy," "frankness," and other themes which have become buzz words in recent years. What I'm suggesting is allowing the reality in you to touch the reality in those you love and those you work with from day to day. While it is an incredibly powerful tool for getting people to do things you want them to do, it cannot be instituted as a policy nor used as a tool for manipulation.

Most people can spot a phony from a mile away.

But genuine openness creates a nurturing climate and sets in motion a whole new set of interpersonal dynamics. Let's look at some ways it does that.

It Wipes Away The We/They Atmosphere —
"Every man is a potential adversary, even those whom
we love," says Dr. Reuel L. Howe.[1] "Only through
dialogue are we saved from this enmity toward one
another...Indeed, this is the miracle of dialogue: it can
bring a relationship into being, and it can bring into
being once again a relationship that has died."

Dr. Howe defined "dialogue" as "getting into significant touch with another person."

This stripping away the masks, this mutual giving
and receiving of our deepest selves, has the power to
transform enemies into friends. It holds the key to
unlocking the doors to the most troublesome relationships: whether in our families, our careers, or among
the superpowers of the world.

We're all in this thing we call life together. When we
get real enough to open our lives to others, we can wipe
away the "they" from our we/they relationships.

It Transforms Fear Into Trust — "Territorial im-
perative" is a term psychologists have used to describe
how we feel compelled to protect ourselves from people
who intrude into our space.

When others approach us, we watch them for clues as
to why they're approaching and what powers they have
to hurt us. The closer they come, the greater our
discomfort grows. If they get too close too quickly, we
either bristle up for a fight, or run away.

Getting real transforms fear into trust and creates
a bridge to others.

It is only when another person reveals his or her
deepest intentions toward us, and we can see they

mean us no harm, that we can let down our guard and receive them into the sacred grounds of our being. Getting real transforms fear into trust and creates a bridge to others.

It Generates Hope — Everywhere I go these days, I see people who are desperately searching for something - anything - they can really believe in.

With newscasts sounding more like horror shows, forecasts of economic disaster, and massive changes avalanching in upon us, reasons for hope seem pretty scarce for many people.

Finding someone of a kindred spirit sparks hope like a glimmer of light in a darkened cave.

It's not as if we have to have all the answers to the many perplexities which plague a hopeless person. They might even reject our answers. Rather, our realness makes them feel less alone.

It Provides A Point Of Contact — For all our technology, ours is an appallingly disconnected world. You can pick up your telephone and easily ring up a dozen people, in as many countries around the world, for a conference call. Yet far too many people find it a lot easier to reach out than to touch someone — even the one they love most deeply.

In a world where people increasingly talk to computers and are mercilessly bombarded by the mass media, responsiveness is indeed a rare commodity. Loneliness stalks the teeming streets of our giant cities and haunts the quiet back roads of rural America.

You see them all the time - people with fixed stares, bumping into thousands of others in crowded airports, on frantic freeways, in bustling offices - everywhere. They touch but don't feel; they hear but don't listen;

they look but don't see; they speak — sometimes even
scream — but no one notices.

Yet call them by name in a tone which says "I care,"
and something wonderful happens. Sure, they'll test
you at first to see if you really mean it. But soon they'll
begin to open up like a rose, one delicate petal at a
time.

It Inspires Cooperation — Most of us have begun
to at least suspect that we simply cannot get all we
really want out of life unless a lot of people help us do
it. The awesome fact is that we need other people.

But they all seem so caught up in their own needs
and desires! Sometimes it seems as if we're not even
there. Executives get excuses instead of production;
salespeople have doors slammed in their faces; custom-
ers have to wait in long lines and often don't get what
they order.

However, getting real with people can often do
wonders to make them want to cooperate with us. It
doesn't always work, but then nothing always works in
human relationships.

Just try it, sometime. You'll be amazed at what
happens! Show a tired and frazzled waitress you really
understand how she feels. Use her name, then express
your gratitude for the service you're receiving. Almost
always, the transaction between you will take on a
whole new character. Your sincere expression of
understanding will usually create an atmosphere of
more cooperation.

To Sum It All Up

It's powerful, this inner connection by getting real. It's the best way I know to become successful in today's world. We've identified getting real as:
- Living "Without Wax."
- Recognizing True Value.
- Coming To Grips With People Potential.
- Becoming Our Own Person.
- Allowing Others To Be Themselves.

And we've seen that it helps us become more effective in all our relationships because:
- It Wipes Away The We/They Atmosphere.
- It Transforms Fear Into Trust.
- It Generates Hope.
- It Provides A Point Of Contact.
- It Inspires Cooperation.

Looking Ahead

That little butterfly who struggled out of her cocoon that day in 1982, while speaking to a medical society, has done much more than flex her wings. She's discovered she's really an eagle.

I can't wait to share with you some of the exiting things which have happened in my life as I've begun my journey in connecting with people. What's more important, I can't wait until you begin to discover more of what a fantastic person you are!

However, I'll try to restrain my enthusiasm while you plunge into your own think-tank to explore how you can use what you've discovered in this opening chapter and prepare yourself for what's coming.

Application Exercise
Focus On Getting Real

Part 1. Getting Real Is . . .

A. Identify one person in your life you feel is most "real." What are the characteristics of that person that make you feel that way?

B. What characteristics are you exhibiting now that show you are real?

C. What actions are you willing to commit to in order to become more real?

Part 2. Why Is Getting Real so Powerful?

A. List some ways you've been positively affected by people whom you felt were real:

B. List some ways you've affected other people by being real with them:

1. Howe, Dr. Reuel L., *The Miracle of Dialogue*, Copyright 1963 by Seabury Press, New York.

Two

Stop the World,
I Want to Get On

Objectives

1. To learn how discovering the real you can enrich your life and boost your effectiveness.

2. To learn why getting real is so risky.

3. To discover five strategies which can help you discover the real you.

People who feel good about themselves produce good results.

— Blanchard and Johnson
The One Minute Manager

Identity Crisis

"What kind of dog have you got there, Elmo?" asks Dagwood in one of the all-time classic comic strips.

"He's a Mexican hairless," explains the little fellow who is holding a very shaggy dog.

"Why does he have so much hair if he's a hairless dog?" asks the somewhat befuddled Dagwood.

"He grew it before he knew what he was!" Elmo explains.

— From "Blondie," by Young and Drake

Maybe you're like many of us who "grew a lot of hair" before we discovered who we really were. In fact, some of us are still discovering what and who we are, and probably always will be learning more about ourselves.

"Normal," "ordinary," "no major problems." Those are the kinds of terms it takes to describe my growing-up years. I was born and raised in a middle-class Italian catholic family on the west side of Chicago. My dad was office manager for Republic Pictures, the movie studio that discovered the likes of John Wayne and Roy Rogers. So, I guess you could say we lived comfortably. Our lives centered around family and neighborhood friends. Mom was the typical, effervescent Italian mama who was loving and giving and chose to see only the best in people. Food was love and she could serve a dozen people a full-course dinner at almost a moment's notice and before the days of microwave ovens.

Home was lots of fun! My two sisters, my brother and I had a lot of day-to-day contact with our parents. They were not able to give us a great deal of future direction because of their own limited backgrounds, but they did encourage us to excel in the realm of traditional roles. Since I was a girl, I never gave much thought to my future. Although I knew I was an achiever, I didn't know how to direct it. I guess it was assumed I'd someday get married, raise a big family and be taken care of by a capable man.

The idea of a "real career" seemed so remote, I never thought about it. So when I was offered a scholarship to nursing school, I jumped at it — not because I wanted be a nurse, but because it was the thing to do. It was a profession I could always "fall back on." I'm so grateful I loved it and that it started me on a path of service and interest in people.

There was a great big wonderful world out there, just waiting for me to tap into it. But, for me, it might as well not have existed — I just didn't know it was there!

In fact, there was a lot about life I didn't know; I simply followed all the stereotypes and did what I thought good people were supposed to do. I studied hard, made top grades and was proud to be the first person in my extended family to complete an education beyond high school.

I married a promising young man, moved to Bowling Green, Kentucky, and settled down to a routine married life. He taught at the university, I worked in management as a nurse at the local hospital and we got busy accumulating all the things a prosperous young couple is supposed to collect.

All this should have made me ecstatically happy, or so I thought. Yet, there was an unsettling feeling growing deep inside: a restlessness; and emptiness; a sense of futility. It was not something I could talk about because I "should have" been happy, and it seemed ungracious to even bring it up. There was a terrible conflict between what I "should be" and what I was feeling. Not knowing how to deal with this conflict, like one of the horses on the plush Kentucky farms, I jumped the fence and ran away from it all. I left the sumptuous new house we'd built, the 100-acre farm, the country clubs — everything.

I headed north to Louisville, and when I arrived, I had to start from scratch. Going from having so much to having so little was quite an adjustment, and it soon became a real struggle just to keep food on the table.

But there was one thing I did bring with me to Louisville; low self-esteem. Tremendous feelings of guilt, a sense of failure, feelings of rejection and isolation all stalked me night and day. All that, added to the struggle for survival, made for some tough years.

Self-esteem is the greatest determining factor in our success or failure in life.

I understood enough about psychology to know that a person's self esteem — one's feeling about self — is probably the greatest determining factor in our success or failure in life. But I felt like a helpless victim, a person who'd been misused and misdirected by people, circumstances and life in general.

Soon, my feelings of aloneness became almost unbearable and I married again. Like most unions based on the wrong reasons it didn't last but a short time. What few resources I'd been able to gather were used up in that brief period, and once again I found myself starting over with nothing.

Why am I telling you all this? I don't even know you!

But then, maybe I do! If we could just sit down and talk for awhile, you could probably tell me some equally painful stories about yourself; perhaps some even more painful. Maybe this little glimpse into my life can help you know that I understand where you're coming from.

I guess the biggest reason I'm sharing all this with you is that I've made some fantastic discoveries about who I am and I want you to know just how powerful those discoveries are. Perhaps knowing where I started from in rebuilding my own life will spark within you the hope that they'll work for you.

* * * * *

Up 'til now, I've been telling you about me. I'll continue to share myself throughout this book, but for now let's talk about you.

Who are you? What kind of person are you? Where are you going? What's the real meaning of your life?

If you have difficulty answering questions like those, you're in for some exciting discoveries. I'm going to share with you some valuable insights about how discovering the real you can enrich your life and boost your personal and professional effectiveness.

All of us have some valuable treasure locked up within us which we can only use when we know who we are and where we're going.

Self-Discovery Treasure #1: It Takes The Pressure Off

There's no greater burden than having to always put up a front; trying to make others believe the best about you, when you're not really sold on yourself.

Psychologists say that the people we usually identify as "having big egos" really don't like themselves much at all. In fact, the more people brag or seek to be the center of attention, the less confident they feel in their own identity. It's like whistling while you walk by a cemetery alone at night — it doesn't do away with the corpses, but it keeps you from hearing all the strange sounds you fear.

Others of us express feelings of inferiority by going to the other extreme: we just withdraw and hope no one will notice we're around. After all, the less people examine you, the less likely they are to find something they don't like.

Still others spend most of their lives trying to run from the pain of not knowing, or not liking, themselves. They may become workaholics, or try to escape into drugs, or alcohol, or frantic activity, or watch television, or take excessive amounts of sleep, or some other form of temporary relief.

Maybe your approach is more like mine has been — always looking for someone who could make me feel like a whole person. There's that nagging feeling that you're only half a person, and the other half of you is bound up in someone else. Thus, you constantly search for your identity by trying to become half of a couple. Unfortunately, people who don't feel complete within themselves put so much pressure on a relationship that they destroy it before it gets started.

But discovering who you really are relieves all that pressure. People who know at a very deep level who they are and what they want out of life are free from all the pressure to constantly explain or justify their actions to themselves and others. They're released from the pressure of always having to prove something.

If you find you're always trying to prove yourself - to your self and to others - you can greatly enrich your life by discovering the real you. Later, we'll explore how you can do just that.

Self-Discovery Treasure #2: It Helps You Concentrate Your Energies On What Really Matters

People who get life sorted out and know where they're going can direct all their energies toward what's most important in their lives.

Knowing who you're not helps you know what you don't want in your life.

Knowing *who you're not* helps you know *what you don't want* in your life. So you don't waste your most creative energies trying to find something which will make you feel worthwhile as a person.

Once you can focus all your attention on what really matters, you'll be amazed at how much of what's important you can get done.

Self-Discovery Treasure #3: It Helps You Communicate What You Want From Others

Peter Drucker, who's been called "the father of American management." says that more than 80 percent of our problems in managing people can be traced to poor communication.

The fact is that most of us have difficulty expressing what we really want from others, and what we want out of our relationships with them. It's not just true in our professional lives; it's true in every area of our lives.

Perhaps the biggest reason we cannot communicate who we are to others is that we, ourselves, don't really know who we are.

The more clearly you can see yourself, the easier it is to communicate your personhood and desires to others.

Why Is it So Hard to Get Real With Ourselves?

From the gods comes the saying "Know thyself," the ancient Greek poet and philosopher Juvenal wrote.[1]

But the Hebrew prophet Jeremiah expressed more accurately what most of us feel when he said: "The heart is deceitful above all things...Who can know it?"[1]

It's not easy, this discovering ourselves. In fact, many of us are like the mythical Prometheus who changed himself into so many different creatures he forgot who he really was. We've played so many roles in our search for finding our true identity that we tend to identify ourselves by what we do, rather than who we are.

Why is it so hard for us to know ourselves, get real about who we are and what we want out of life?

It seems as if clouds surround our innermost thoughts so we cannot see ourselves as we really are. But what are those clouds which hide our own self-discovery?

Self-Discovery Cloud #1: Fear of Rejection

Many scientific studies have found that most of us fear being rejected more than we fear even death itself. Something deep within us seems to say, "They must not see me as I really am, or they will reject me."

So we play games with others. It's not at all unusual for us to be one thing with a certain person or group, and something entirely different with others.

Yet the measures we take to ensure that others don't see us as we really are seem small when compared with what we will do to hide from ourselves.

It's easier to wander around in confusion than to face the possibility of discovering ourselves to be something we might hold in contempt — a person we would reject.

Thus, we focus all our attention on things we "ought to do," and on the way we're "supposed to feel." We hide from what we want to do, and what we really feel.

We become unreal because we demand perfection from ourselves as the only thing which could make us lovable. And we dare not face the possibility of being unlovable.

So we constantly compare ourselves with our ideals and with other people and find we come up short. To shield us from the pain of what we think we might be, we convince ourselves that we are something we wish we could be.

Ultimately, it's a game we cannot win.

Self-Discovery Cloud #2: Fear Of Failure

Fear of failure often keeps us from discovering who we really are. A number of studies have confirmed that more than half of all adults dislike their careers or professions, yet most say they have no plans to change.

"Play it safe!" we tell ourselves. It's risky business to change from something we hate but have come to depend upon and to launch out into strange territory. So we take the easy way out and stay put.

In most cases, playing it safe means doing what others expect, or want, us to do. Maybe it's because we are looking to others to protect us from failure, to provide for us, and to make our decisions for us. Then, if things go wrong, we can always blame someone else. If we are unhappy, we can always say it's their fault.

So we look around to see what our peers are doing, then try to copy it. We imagine what others want us to be, and set about to convince them that's what we are.

Thus we settle into roles we think others want us to play, even though we may hate playing these roles. We begin acting according to the labels others pin on us, even though we feel deep inside that they don't really fit us. What's even worse is that we begin believing we are nothing more than others expect us to be.

Some of us get so caught up in the stereotypes that we lose sight of all the dreams we once had. As I go about all over the county speaking, I meet an enormous number of people who tell me they have no idea what they want to do with their lives. Yet many of them find it easier to blame their unhappiness on other people, or their circumstance, than to risk failure. So they dare not even dream about what their lives could be.

I've discovered that fixing the blame for all that's wrong in your life is far less satisfying than fixing whatever keeps you from becoming who you really are.

Self-Discovery Cloud #3: Feelings Of Guilt

Feelings of guilt are so subtle that most of us don't even realize we have them. "I haven't done anything wrong!" we shout when someone suggests guilt may be present.

But that kind of guilt is not the issue here. It's usually pretty obvious to us that if we've committed some gross "evil, " we cannot begin to become real until we deal with the guilt it creates within us.

The issue I'm raising is the feelings of guilt which come from making decisions and choices which force us into an unreal existence.

Life demands that we decide; all day, every day. To choose one value is often to say no the other values.

We may make a choice that we later discover was not the best for us. Or we may choose to act, again and again, in a manner that is not in keeping with the way we see ourselves.

We may consciously justify our decisions and choices but subconsciously we tend to feel we must be either dumb or terrible. Thus it becomes easier to believe all the worst about ourselves than it is to believe the good we suspect may be there.

We develop the habit of thinking negatively about ourselves; of blaming ourselves for not measuring up to our own ideals; of constantly putting ourselves down.

Some of us may even nourish the notion that everything bad that happens to us is some form of punishment for being the kinds of people we are.

Let me give you one of Elizabeth's laws: If you feel rotten about yourself, your self-esteem is based on false information. When you discover the real you, you'll understand what I mean.

Self-Discovery Cloud #4: Closing Others Out

One of the strange paradoxes of life is that no one else can make us who we are, yet we can only be ourselves when we allow others into our lives. While we are not half-persons who can only find our other half in someone else, we cannot truly discover our real selves until we let others into our lives at a very deep level.

Yet no other area of our lives causes us as much pain as our relationships with other people. Sometimes our pain is brought on by our own actions toward others. At other times it's because someone else has hurt us by their rejection of us, or by something they've done to us.

Rejection and abuse hurt, so we move to protect ourselves. "No one will ever hurt me like that again!"

we firmly vow. When someone tries to get into our hearts, we close them out. If we don't let them matter to us, we reason, then they can't hurt us.

We erect elaborate walls to keep others from getting close to us: walls like anger, withdrawal, apathy (an "I don't care" attitude), and grudges. For a while, we feel safe.

But sooner or later, we discover that the walls we've built to protect us from others have become our prison. They distort our view of ourselves, and discolor our view of others.

Whatever else we may survive without, we need people. This need for others begins with the first breath we draw; it influences everything we do during our whole lives; it's still present the moment we draw our final breath. None of us can make it alone.

So we feel trapped between our need for people and our fears about letting them into our deepest selves.

Self-Discovery Cloud #5: Denying Our Spirituality

There is a spiritual dimension to our lives which must be dealt with before we can really discover who we are. We may choose to ignore it, or neglect it, or even to fight against it, but that won't make it go away.

We tend to focus most of our day-to-day attention on what we call "the real world" of things we can see, touch, hear, smell and taste. Those things have a way of pressing us for decisions, forcing us to take actions, and shaping our feelings.

But our spiritual dimension is not so routinely de-manding. In fact, spiritual development has to be actively pursued — often at the expense of material concerns. It's something you have to desire and work toward, or it just doesn't develop as a vital part of your life.

None of us can ever really know ourselves until we have faced up to the question of what we will do about our relationship with God.

Yet, none of us can ever really know ourselves until we have faced up to the question of what we will do about our relationship with God.

Five Strategies for Discovering the Real You

These five clouds surround our real personhood until we face up to them and take concrete actions to clear them away. It is only when you actively remove those clouds that you can begin to really discover who you are and what your life is all about.

But what can you do about the inner confusion which keeps you from discovering the real you? How can you clear away the fog which keeps you from becoming all you were created to be?

I want to share with you five strategies for discovering who you are — one of for each of the clouds.

Self-Discovery Strategies
- Take responsibility for your own life.
- Accept yourself as you are, and go from there.
- Believe in yourself.
- Target your life.
- Keep your life in balance.

Believe me, these five tactics really work! They're not empty theories; they've been tested and proven in the laboratory of my own life and the lives of countless other people. I believe they'll work for you.

In fact, these strategies have proven so effective in my own life that I'd like to invest a whole chapter exploring each of them and how they can work for you.

Maybe some of the clouds are more pronounced in your life than are the others. Perhaps you've already started clearing away some of them. However, I've found it very helpful to keep refocusing who I am and what I really want out of life,. This is how we all continue to grow.

To Sum It All Up

Do you ever have the feeling that there's something about yourself you haven't yet discovered? It's like your life is a jigsaw puzzle with a key piece missing.

In this chapter, we've seen:

1. How discovering the real you can enrich your life and boost your effectiveness.

2. Why getting real is so scary.

3. Five strategies which can help you discover the real you.

Before we jump into the first of the five strategies, let me suggest you spend some time reflecting on the "Application Exercise," which is designed to help you explore your own feelings about discovering yourself.

Application Exercise
Focus On Self-Discovery

Part 1. Boosting Your Effectiveness Through Self-Discovery

A.   Do you ever feel pressured to do things that are inconsistent with the way you see yourself? If so, list the ones which you feel most often:

B.   Specifically, what positive outcomes could you anticipate if you knew yourself at a deeper level?

Part 2. Why Getting Real Is So Risky

A. Are there some things you do (don't do) because you fear others might reject you? List the ones you most dislike:

B. Do you ever feel that fear of failure keeps you from trying new things? If so, list some things you'd like to do.

C. Do you ever wish you could be more open with certain people? If so, list some of them and tell how you'd like to be able to get more open:

Person   Ways You'd Like To Be More Open

E. Describe some ways you'd like to deepen the spiritual dimension of your life:

1.   Juvenalis, Decimus Junius, Satires, reference *The Oxford Dictionary of Quotations*, Second Edition, Copyright 1955 by Oxford University Press, London, page 12.

2.   Jeremiah 17:9, *The Bible*, King James Version.

ELIZABETH   JEFFRIES

Three

Take Full Responsibility for Your Own Life

Objectives

1. To discover what it means to take charge of your own life.

2. To connect with your inner resources for taking charge.

3. To learn how to take charge of your own life.

If it is to be, It is up to me!

— Anonymous

All Right, Who's in Charge Here?

When you were a little kid, would you agree that someone else always took responsibility for you?

Maybe you didn't like it when others were always telling you what to do, but there were certain benefits to the arrangement.

First, you didn't have to fend for yourself; you could spend all your time on important things like having fun, and getting what you wanted.

Second, you didn't have to make a lot of decisions. You might not always have liked what others decided, but at least you didn't have to struggle with making a lot of life-and-death choices. Besides, if you were clever enough, you could bend many of the decisions others made to your own advantage.

Third, and perhaps most significant, you didn't have to take responsibility for the way things turned out. If you were unhappy, you could blame someone else, or circumstances beyond your control. You could even wriggle your way out of tight spots by making excuses.

Now you're running your own life! You can go where you want to go, do what you want to do, and be what you want to be.

You're completely in charge! Or, are you?

Maybe you're a little like I was - wanting my independence, yet way down inside hoping someone else was going to take care of me, and always blaming others or my circumstances for everything that was wrong in my life.

Or maybe you're one of the many people who're always blaming themselves and feeling as if they can't do anything right.

But that's all in the past, now!

It's time to quit blaming...
- Others
- Circumstances
- Yourself!

Fixing the blame is a child's game; fixing our life is the only worthwhile goal.

What it Means to Take Charge of Your Own Life

"I did it my way!" Frank Sinatra's big hit song proudly boasted. Perhaps one reason the song has been so popular for so long is that most people like to feel they are doing things their way. Yet the facts seem to indicate that the opposite is true of most people:

- There are an estimated five million alcoholics, and an additional five to seven million "problem drinkers" in America today — not to mention the millions of people who are dependent on some form of drugs.

- More than half of all working adults hate their jobs.

- More people than ever are depending upon the government for some form of assistance.

- The number of suicides annually has more than doubled within the last 10 years.

Of course, those are broad figures about people in general. But we're not talking about people in general — we're talking about you and me.

You can tell you're not taking full responsibility for yourself when:

1. You feel your happiness, emotional well-being, or identity depends upon another person or a set of circumstances: you are chronically depressed, bored

or unhappy and feel there is nothing you can do about it.

2. You think your financial security depends upon what others do, or upon certain events.

3. You often find it more attractive to take the easy way out when confronted with a tough challenge or problem.

4. You feel you are frequently the victim of forces beyond your control.

5. You allow others to determine your moods by nursing anger, grudges, and thoughts of getting even.

6. Destructive or negative habits constantly make you do things that are inconsistent with the way you see yourself.

7. You stay in a job or a set of circumstances you don't like, rather than taking the risks necessary to make a change.

8. You find it easy to blame others or circumstances for making your life miserable, for mistakes you make, or for failing to do your best.

9. You find it increasingly hard to get yourself motivated to do things you have decided are in your best interest.

10.You often find yourself looking to others to make decisions for you.

These are only a few of the symptoms that indicate you're not really in control of your own life. You can probably think of some others, too. The important thing is to constantly be alert for any indication that you are looking to someone or something to shape your life, and deal with it for what it really is. So what do I mean when I say discovering the real you begins when you start taking full responsibility for your own life?

Taking Charge of Your Life

Taking full responsibility for your life means: **Recognizing that you are where you want to be, doing what you want to do, or you'd change it.** It means you quit blaming others, circumstances, or yourself for things you don't like and set about to change them.

Taking charge is becoming self-reliant. It means you look first to yourself, instead of always looking to others to take care of you. It's learning how to draw on your own inner resources.

> *Taking responsibility for yourself is making things happen instead of waiting for something to happen.*

Taking responsibility for yourself is making things happen instead of waiting for something to happen. It's acting positively to achieve goals that are important to you, instead of simply reacting to whatever comes up.

It's doing what you really want to do instead of always doing what others think you ought to do. Taking charge is building your life the way you want it, instead of allowing the opinions of others to shape all your decisions.

It's making your own choices and facing up to your own consequences. Being responsible for yourself is making rational decisions, based on solid information, and committing yourself in advance to bear whatever burden those decisions may produce.

Taking responsibility is being willing to forego the fun-for-the-moment experiences in order to achieve long-term goals. It's exercising whatever self-discipline is needed to make your dreams become realities. In short, what we're talking about is growing up and acting in your own best interest, then enjoying your own success or facing up to your own failures.

Connecting With Your Own Inner Resources

Right now, I've got some good news, and I've got some bad news for your. The bad news is that you're all you've got. There's not going to be any Superman or Superwoman to rescue you from your low self-esteem or negative circumstances. Nobody can change your life but you. But the good news is that you're all you need! Once you firmly decide to take charge of your own life, you'll discover you have inner resources greater than you ever dreamed possible. You can cope with whatever life sends your way, and you can make your life all you really want it to be.

When you start putting all your weight down on your own two shoulders, you'll discover they're the shoulders you've always wanted to lean on. And you'll also discover they are much stronger than you had thought. That little voice way down inside you that keeps whispering "There's more to you than you've thought!" is right. So isn't it about time to quit blaming others and circumstances for your troubles and take full responsibility for your own life? I promise that once you do, you'll begin to make some fantastic discoveries about yourself; you'll begin to discover the real you.

Take-Charge Resource #1: Your Mind

Maybe you don't thing of yourself as a brilliant person, but you might be surprised at just how much brain power you have. According to the UCLA Brain Research Institute, the average brain has an almost limitless capacity to create, store, and learn. "Throughout our lives we use only a fraction of our thinking ability," a Soviet brain specialist once said. "We could, without any difficulty whatever, learn forty languages, memorize a set of encyclopedias from A to Z, and complete the required course of dozens of colleges."[1] The limiting factor is not your mind: it's your attitude about learning and using your mind. "Whatever the mind of man (or woman) can conceive and believe it can achieve," wrote Napoleon Hill.[2]

What it all means is that your mind will give you all the knowledge and wisdom you need to take full responsibility for your own life. But, obviously, the more you cultivate your brain power the more completely you can take charge.

Take-Charge Resource #2: Your Will

"Most people are about as happy as they make up their minds to be," said Abraham Lincoln. I've discovered he's right, and a whole lot more. I'd say "Most people are just about anything they make up their minds to be."

One Saturday morning, Arnold Lemerand was taking a leisurely stroll when he saw a small child pinned beneath an 1,800-lb. clay pipe on a construction site.

Lemerand, age 56, looked around for someone to help but there was no one in sight. Realizing that the small boy would soon die unless rescued, he did the only thing he could do — he reached down and lifted the huge pipe off the little fellow's head. Later, he tried to lift that pipe but could not budge it.

In a follow-up story, the Associated Press reported that Lemerand was far from a weight lifter. Six years before he broke the world record for lifting this 1800-lb. weight, he had suffered a severe heart attack. "I try to avoid heavy lifting," Lemerand told a reporter.

You will never know what you can do until you have to do something that is beyond all the limits you have previously set for yourself. At that moment, you will discover the tremendous power of your own will.

Actually, people who take charge of their own lives frequently find themselves doing things they never thought they could do — simply because they want badly enough to do them.

Take-Charge Resource #3: Your Body

In its own way, your body is as great a resource for taking charge of your life as is your mind or your will.

It's easy for any of us to see how we can use our hands or our feet to do things that will make us a living. But our bodies contain far more potential than simply manipulating tools or machines.

Your body houses eyes which give you the power to see beyond the obvious; ears to hear the sounds which can open almost unimaginable doors for you; a mouth which can communicate your most vital messages, etc.

The capacities of the human body exceed our wildest expectations, once we learn how to use it. It has built-in mechanisms to heal itself, renew itself — even to control its own weight. All our systems are designed to work together in perfect harmony.

Unfortunately, most people tend to think of their bodies as nothing more than a place to be. As you explore its capacities, you will be amazed at all the resources it will give you for making your life what you want it to be.

Take-Charge Resource #4: Your Emotions

Up until now, you might have thought of your emotions more as a liability than an asset. I hope you'll break away from such an idea because your emotions are a tremendous resource for getting what you want out of life.

The problem arises when we try to force our "ought to's" upon the "want to's" of our subconscious mind. They rebel and become a tremendous hindrance to whatever we're trying to do.

But when our deepest desires are in harmony with our conscious and rational ideas, they create a synergy which is powerful beyond belief. A synergy is where the whole is greater than the sum of its parts. It's where you add two and two and get eight.

"Through some strange and powerful principle of 'mental chemistry' which she has never divulged, Nature wraps up in the impulse of strong desire 'that something' which recognizes no such word as impossible, and accepts no such reality as failure," said Napoleon Hill.[3]

As you learn to use your emotions as a propelling force, rather than constantly fighting with them, you will have discovered a tremendous resource for taking charge of your own life.

Take-Charge Resource #5: Your Spirit

God placed within each of us a spirit which makes us as far above the lower animals as the sky is above the tallest building. It's what gives us our capacity to love, to have faith and hope, and to keep going when everything in our human make-up wants to quit.

The God-spirit within us energizes our highest resources; it constantly calls us to become more than we have ever been; it enables us so we can give freely what no one can take from us. It's that force within which urges us to create, to remain responsive in an unresponsive world, and to care for those who hurt.

Perhaps even more exciting is the fact that our spirit gives us the ability to connect with God and to marshall all his infinite resources. Thus it assures us that we are never completely alone, gives us the quiet inner confidence that nothing can overwhelm us, and enables us to operate at levels beyond our natural capacity. You'll find your spirit to be a valuable and constantly reliable resource for taking charge of your own life.

How to Take Charge of Your Own Life

We've explored what it means to take responsibility for your own life and some of the resources you have for doing it. But how do you do it?

Ultimately, no one can tell you exactly how to do it in your own life, precisely because it's up to you to decide. However, there are some clues I've found very helpful; some actions which might give you a new sense of direction and control of your own life.

Take-Charge Clue #1: Life Is Difficult

"Life is difficult," said Dr. M. Scott Peck. "It is a
great truth because once we really see this truth, we
transcend it. Once we really know that life is difficult -
once we truly understand and accept it — then life is
no longer difficult. Because once it is accepted, the fact
that life is difficult no longer matters."[4]

Maybe you're like so many of us who grew up thinking that life was supposed to be all fun, that the world
was "fair" that there would always be someone to look
out for us; and that most problems would just go away.

We live in a culture which encourages us to think
that way. We are bombarded with ads and commercials
telling us that pain is not only unnecessary but stupid,
that our deepest needs can be met by buying "things,"
and that we "deserve" to pamper ourselves. The news
media would lead us to believe that all our problems
come from failures in government, that complex questions have only two sides, and that somebody always
owes us something.

The problem with that kind of thinking is that it
creates false expectations and leads us to always be
looking for the easy way out.

> *Once we really face up to the fact that life is
> difficult, we learn to look to our own resources
> and find them more than adequate.*

But once we really face up to the fact that life is
difficult, we learn to look to our own resources and
find them more than adequate. We discover that it is
through pain and struggle that we learn and grow, that
problems are really opportunities in disguise, and that
we can cope with whatever life sends our way.

It is only when we approach life as a constant challenge, that we can really savor the sweet taste of victory and become the magnificent creatures we were designed to be.

Take-Charge Clue #2: Freedom Always Contains Risk

Freedom basically means not being under another's control. It's the ability to choose for ourselves — even when our choices are not in our best interest. But choosing always involves risk. To say "yes" to one possibility always means saying "no" to whatever possibilities are in conflict with our choice.

What's more, our choices always carry consequences with them. And sometimes the seriousness of those consequence seems far out of proportion to the choices we make, For example, it may seem a simple thing to drive home after drinking too much at a cocktail party, but the results can destroy others' lives and radically alter ours.

Therefore, taking charge of your own life always means accepting responsibility for the choices you make.

Take-Charge Clue #3: The Key to Self-Discipline Is Desire

We grow up and get out on our own because we want to do things our way, yet, if we mature, we often find ourselves doing freely many of the things we were once forced to do.

Unfortunately, all too often we see our growing up as an escape from the discipline of others, rather than the establishment of our own self-control. Thus we develop habits, like always opting for the immediate pleasure instead of delaying it for a greater pleasure, and we bring untold pain upon ourselves by our efforts to escape pain.

It is only when we quit looking for the easy way out and the quick fix that we can begin to discover who we really are and move toward our full potential.

The key to all self-discipline is desire.

What we're talking about is self-discipline; taking the long view of life; taking responsibility; constantly searching for truth and integrity; the balancing of goals and values.

The key to all self-discipline is desire. The athlete who trains endlessly, the business leader who refuses to cheat, and the worker who does his or her best even when no one is looking, all have one thing in common: they desire to be their best. Thus, discipline comes from the inside out; it's an automatic response to their overpowering desire to be all that they can be.

It is only when your "ought to's" and your "want to's" are in harmony with your deepest desires that you can exercise complete self-control.

Take-Charge Clue #4: Life's Greatest Limits Are Self-Imposed

Limitations imposed upon us by others or by circumstances are usually obvious to us, and often draw our greatest attention. We look for ways of breaking free from them; but, if we are unsuccessful, we usually try to find ways of getting around them.

Yet the real limits of life most often come from within us — not from the outside. Others may tell us we can't do something, but it is only when we believe we can't that we don't at least give it a try. Circumstances may look overwhelming, but they can only overwhelm us when we accept them as bigger than ourselves. Likewise, others may try to put us down and belittle our abilities, but as Eleanor Roosevelt said, "No one can make you feel inferior without your permission."

"We have met the enemy, and he is us!" Walt Kelly's great philosopher Pogo once exclaimed. It's really true! We are our own worst enemies and our greatest limiting factors.

It is only when we constantly remind ourselves that life's greatest limits are self-imposed that we can overcome whatever external obstacles we must to take charge of our own lives.

Take-Charge Clue #5: Some Loneliness Is Inevitable

We humans are social creatures and craving the warmth of the herd is as natural for us as is breathing. We want to be loved, accepted, and affirmed. In a later chapter, we're going to discover just how important our relationships with others are.

Yet, taking charge of your own life inevitably leads to some loneliness. That which makes us the unique and wonderful creatures we are sets us apart from all others. Actually, the word "unique" means "one of a kind."

Breaking away from your peers to become your own person will always produce a feeling of aloneness. Some will not agree with your choices, and they may quietly reject you or openly criticize your decisions — especially when your choices conflict with their desires for you.

The more you grow and the greater you become, the less you can expect to be understood.

In fact, the more you grow and the greater you become, the less you can expect to be understood. "To be great is to be misunderstood," said Emerson.[5]

Seeking wise counsel from others may prove very helpful at times, but ultimately you must make your own choices in every area of life. Learning to trust your own judgment, to rely upon your own experiencing process, and to act as you see best may lead to some loneliness, but it is the only way you can become the magnificent person you were destined to be. The acceptance of these concepts was a new beginning for me. I think it can be for you, too.

To Sum It All Up

In this chapter, I've sought to enable you:

1. To discover what it means to take charge of your own life.

2. To connect with your inner resources for taking charge.

3. To learn how to take charge of your own life.

May I suggest you spend some time working through the following "Application Exercise," exploring how some of the insights you've gained can enable you to more effectively take responsibility for yourself.

Application Exercise
Taking Charge Of Your Own Life

Who's In Charge Here?

A. Are you now where you want to be, doing what you want to do in all areas of your life?   Yes __   No __.

If not, how would you like to change your life?

B. Have you experienced the victory of delaying a pleasure to achieve a more long-term goal?   List some goals and tell how you reached them by delaying pleasures:

Long-Term Goal   Pleasure Delayed

C. What actions are you willing to commit to in assuming more responsibility for your own life?

1. Yefremov, Ivan, quoted by Earl Nightingale on "Our Changing World" (radio program). Copyright August 1974, by Nightingale-Conant, Inc., Chicago.

2. Hill, Napoleon, *Think and Grow Rich*, Copyright 1937 by Napoleon Hill, Revised Edition published by Fawcett Publications, Inc., Greenwich, Conn., page 32.

3. Ibid, page 47.

4. Peck, M. Scott, M.D., *The Road Less Traveled*, copyright 1978 by M. Scott Peck, M.D., published by Simon & Schuster, New York, page 15.

5. Emerson, Ralph Waldo, Self-Reliance, reference The Oxford Dictionary of Quotations, Second Edition, Copyright 1955 by Oxford University Press, London, page 200.

Four

Accept Yourself As You Are, And Go From There

Objectives

1. To discover what it means to accept yourself as you are.

2. To learn how to clear away the distortions from your self-image.

No one can make you feel inferior without your permission.

— Eleanor Roosevelt

The Greatest Obstacle

"If only" may very well be the biggest obstacle you'll
ever have to climb over. Most of us have used that
little phrase as an excuse for not becoming all we were
created to be. If only I had:
- More money.
- More education.
- Better breaks.
- More support.
- Greater opportunities.
- Fewer problems.

If only I had not:
- Made so many mistakes (especially that one).
- Spent so much money.
- Wasted so much of my life on...
- Gotten off to such a bad start.

If only I were:
- Better looking.
- Taller/shorter/thinner.
- Healthier.
- Stronger.
- Smarter.
- A different race/sex/age.

If only I were not:
- Handicapped.
- So unlucky.
- Such a wimp.
- So afraid.

Yes, and if an elephant had wings he'd be a big bird! But he doesn't, and he isn't, and you don't, and you did, and you weren't, and you were! So the elephant walks on all fours! What are you going to do?

Accept yourself, exactly as you are, and go from there.

I have a suggestion that can revolutionize your life. Accept yourself, exactly as you are, and go from there.

Accepting Yourself

To accept means "to receive graciously," to believe in," and all of us can do that. It doesn't mean you have to "approve of" or "like" everything about yourself and your circumstances.

In 1653, Oliver Cromwell was named Lord Protector of England, and was promptly ordered by the king to pose for a portrait. After vigorous protest, he finally submitted and began what he believed a waste of time.

"Sire, could you turn the other way?" requested the artist, noting that Sir Cromwell had a big wart which should not be included in the portrait.

"No!" shouted the crusty old statesman. "You will paint me, warts and all!" There are basically three things involved in accepting yourself:

1. Accept the undesirable things you cannot change.

There are certain limiting factors all of us have, and each of us may have certain additional limitations.

None of us can change our height, our race, our age, our sex (except in rare cases), our past, and many other things. Some of us can't change certain physical handicaps, characteristics, and other things.

Fighting against what we cannot change is useless; feeling sorry for ourselves only makes our burden heavier; fixing the blame does nothing to fix the problems it causes.

But accepting the things we cannot change opens the door to a whole new realm of exciting possibilities. For example, it is foolish to deny that you are aging as you near your seventieth birthday; it is quite another to accept your age and propose to make the most of the rest of your life.

2. Assume full responsibility for changing the undesirable things you can change.

Most of the things which cause us our deepest pains and keep us from reaching our full potential are things we can change. It may not be easy, but each of us can change:

- Our negative and defeating self-image.
- Our lack of self-confidence.
- Our greatest fears and anxieties.
- Destructive roles we play.
- Most of our problems.
- Many of our flaws.
- Damaging habits.
- Our career.
- Where we live.

We can change all those things, and a whole lot more — if we're willing to pay the price. Later, we'll explore how you can change them, and what it will take to change them.

The important thing for now is to assume full responsibility for changing all the undesirable things in your life that you can change.

3. Receive yourself as the wonderful and exciting creature you are.

There's a whole lot more to you than you may realize. Many wonderful and exciting things go into making you the unique creature you are:

- Your unique personality makes you wonderfully different from all others. No one else in the world is quite like you.

- You have a body that is all your own. No one's eyeprints, footprints, fingerprints or voiceprints are exactly like yours.

- Your values are your own and shape many of the things you do.

- You have ideas which set you apart from all others.

- Your interests and desires make you one of a kind.

- Your needs may be similar to the needs of others, but they are different.

- No one else in the whole world can do exactly what you can do.

- You have strengths which many others may wish they had.

Maybe you're so caught up in trying to be like everybody else that you cannot see your unique beauty. Characteristics you would gladly change are often the very traits which go into making you the exciting person you are.

This Little Light of Mine

Most of us find a total eclipse of the sun to be a fascinating phenomenon. The eerie darkness, the strange distortions, the black shadow over the sun's face, and the deathly stillness all combine to create a feeling that we are in an alien world.

But imagine what it would be like to live in that setting all the time. What's interesting, because it is so rare and only lasts for a few minutes, would be devastating to all living and growing creatures if it became a permanent condition.

Preoccupation with things that could be, hides all the exciting and wonderful things that are.

Yet living with the "if only" mentality creates precisely the same shadowing effect within your life. Preoccupation with things that could be, hides all the exciting and wonderful things that are. It keeps you from discovering and developing the greatest things you have going for you.

If you want to see your life really take off, spend some time getting acquainted with the unique and wonderful person you are.

Please quit hiding behind your perceived flaws and let your light shine. This dark world needs the glow you bring.

Remove the Distortions From Your Self-Image

Every related psychological study of the last three decades has confirmed that nothing impacts more greatly on our lives than does our self-image — our own mental portrait and our self-esteem, our feelings about that mental picture. Discovering who you are involves removing all the negative distortions so you can see clearly how wonderful you really are.

Most of our feelings about ourselves are based on such shallow valuing scales as:

- How we look.
- What we have.
- What we can do.

Thus we concern ourselves with:

- How we think others see us.
- How what we have compares with what others have.
- How brilliant (or not so brilliant) we appear to be.

Such measures cannot possibly do justice to the unique and wonderful person we are because they:

- Are based on inadequate and inaccurate measures.
- Focus only on outward appearance.
- Are distorted by false perceptions.

Most of us grossly underestimate our value to ourselves and the world around us.

As a result, most of us grossly underestimate our value to ourselves and the world around us. Let's look at why we often feel so rotten about ourselves.

Self-Image Distortion #1: How We Look

Physical features probably top the list of traits we use to describe ourselves. Yet physical characteristics only form the outer shell of the real person each of us is.

Physical perfection is sought by many, but possessed by none. For example, glamorous singing star Karen Carpenter died in 1983 from the effects of anorexia-nervosa (starvation dieting), despite the fact that she was seriously underweight. Most of Hollywood's most lustrous stars (both male and female) openly admit to having severe doubts about their physical appearances.

There's only one way to win the game of valuing yourself and others by looks — refuse to play it!

Certainly it's wise to look your best, but don't let your perceptions about the way you look shape your sense of value. Look more deeply at such things as your character, your personhood, and what you mean to others.

> *There's only one way to win the game of valuing yourself and others by looks — refuse to play it!*

Self-Image Distortion #2: What We Have

Modern America is the richest, most acquisitive and materialistic culture in the history of the world. Yet, for all our money and possessions, several leading psychologists have described the state of our mental health as "an epidemic of inferiority."

Why, when we have so much, do we feel so rotten about ourselves? It's because we measure our self-worth by what we have, and possessions have nothing to do with our real value as human beings.

Oddly enough, most people would probably agree intellectually with what I have just said. However, what we feel inside often has little to do with the facts, or the way we perceive those facts.

For example, we tend to:

- Seek to emulate "successful (rich) people," even though we say the people we admire most are those who give most freely of themselves to others.

- Define failure as losing our material possessions, or not maintaining the lifestyle our self-image demands.

- Invest our most creative energies in the pursuit of money — often to the point of physical breakdown.

- Worry more about not having enough money than about all other considerations combined — although our definitions of "enough" keep getting bigger and bigger.

Please understand that I'm not being critical. I'm only trying to focus how what we say about money does not always square with how we act in relation to it.

What we do is usually a better indication of how we feel about ourselves, and what we value, than is what we say.

Assess Your Wealth, Not Your Riches — As you seek to discover your true value as a human being, let me suggest you focus more on wealth than on riches. That little play on words contains a secret which can do wonders for your self-esteem.

Our riches include things like how much money we have or make, what material assets we have, and physical comforts we enjoy. This is not to suggest those things are undesirable or evil. Believe me, I've been rich and I've been poor, and I prefer the former!

All I'm suggesting is that riches have nothing to do with your value as a person.

A far greater measure of your self-esteem is how much wealth you have:

- Special people who make you smile and bring joy to your life, and what you bring to them.

- Friends and family who stick with you when life gets tough and believe in you when you seem to falter.

- Your inner resources for coping with whatever life sends your way.

- Your unique creativity, imagination, and insights into life.

- The value system, beliefs, and love which make you the special person you are.

That list could be much longer, but you get the idea, don't you? Most of what really counts in assessing your true value is invisible; it's intangible. Yet any assessment of your worth which is based on anything else can only cause you to undervalue yourself.

And that brings us to the third false standard by which we humans tend to value ourselves.

Self-Image Distortion #3: What We Can Do

John Belushi was widely acclaimed as one the true geniuses in Hollywood, and many thought he would be remembered among the greats like Bogart, Wayne, and Dietrich.

But that brilliant life and career ended tragically and abruptly from a massive overdose of drugs. Biographer Bob Woodward reported[2] that Belushi stayed drunk and doped up most of the time in the months before his death.

What was it that drove this highly capable man to seek such constant and destructive escape? "Fear of failure," is Woodward's simple explanation.

"For days before every filming and every performance this brilliant actor would be so afraid he'd bomb out with the audience that he'd literally come apart," said Woodward.[3]

Fear of failure is not at all unusual for people who assess their value upon what they can do; even if they are extremely good at everything they do. It doesn't always reach such enormous proportions, but it can be a merciless tormentor.

Certainly, all this does not suggest that people who perform at low levels are free from fears of failure, nor even that a person should do less than she or he is capable of doing. What it suggest is that what you can do is a poor measure of your true worth as a human being. In fact, the only way we can reach our full potential as humans, and do all we're capable of doing, is to start from the position of accurately valuing ourselves.

Self-Image Distortion #4: The Way Others Treat Us

Maybe you feel like nothing because someone treats you like nothing. They call you junk, act as if you're junk, and tell others you're junk. But just because you've been treated like you're ready for the trash heap does not mean you're junk. You only become it when you believe it.

You can capture an eagle and put it in a cage. You can call it a chicken; you can hang a sign on the front of the cage that identifies it as a chicken; you can laugh and poke fun at it all day as if it were a chicken which had claimed to be and eagle. But that doesn't make it a chicken.

If by chance you should someday leave the cage door open for just a few moments, that giant bird would quickly bound out of that cage. After a brief pause to gain its bearings, it would flap its huge wings and soar off into the sky — all the while screaming for all the world like an eagle.

Believing all the terrible things others may have said about us can only give us a distorted view of our own identity. What really matters is what you think yourself to be. Remember, *you are what you think you are.*

A far greater scale for estimating your worth is what you are. Self-esteem is not something you earn; it's an appraisal you make of your own value as a human being. "I am, therefore I have value," is a valid way of expressing it.

"Anyone can count the seeds in an apple, but only God can count the apples in a seed," says Dr. Robert Schuller. In the final analysis, all any of us can do is estimate our true value — only God knows for sure how much we're really worth. But I suspect that each of us is far more valuable than we even dare to dream we are.

To Sum It All Up

As a creature made in the image of God, each of us is special in our own way. In this chapter we've sought:

1. To discover what it means to accept yourself as you are.

2. To learn how to clear away the distortions from our self-image — to measure your worth by what you are; not by the false standard of how you look, what you have, what you can do, and how others treat you.

In our next chapter, we'll focus on how to build a more positive self-image and sound self-esteem. But first, take a few moments to apply what you've learned.

Application Exercise
Focus On Self-Image Distortions

1. Do you ever wish you could be someone else? If so, why?

2. Have you ever felt inferior because of the way you look? If so, how can you remove this distortion?

3. Do you find yourself at times comparing what you have or the salary you make with other people ? If so, how can you remove this distortion?

4. Do you ever fear that you will fail and that the failure will make you an inferior person? What can you do to ease this fear?

5. Have you allowed criticism by others to make you dislike yourself? If so, what will you do to clear away the distortion?

1. Brand, Paul Wilson, M.D., and Yancey, Philip, *In His Image*, Copyright 1984 by Paul Brand and Philip Yancey, published by Zondervan Publishing House, Grand Rapids, Mich.

2. Reference; Woodward, Bob, *Wired*, Copyright 1984 by Simon, New York.

3. Reference: Woodward, Bob, interview on "The Donahue Show."

E L I Z A B E T H   J E F F R I E S

Five

Believe in Yourself

Objectives

1. To grasp the awesome power of believing in yourself.

2. To discover how to boost your self-confidence through creative imaging.

3. To learn how to master the art of self-talk.

*Faith is a state of mind which may be induced,
or created, by affirmation or repeated instructions
to the subconscious mind...*

— Napoleon Hill

"You've Come a Long Way, Baby"

"Vilma! Vilma! Vilma!" roared 80,000 fans as Wilma Rudolph walked into the stadium in Rome for the 1960 Olympic Games.

They sensed they were about to see one of those special performances in the tradition of great Olympians like Jesse Owens and Babe Didrikson before her, and Mary Lou Retton and Jackie Joyner-Kersee who would follow.

How right they were! "Vilma" posted three electrifying races: breezing to easy victories in the 100- and 200-meter dashes; anchoring the victory for the U.S. Woman's team for the 400-meter relay. She became the first woman in history to ever win three gold medals, and each of her victories came with world-record times.

Wilma Rudolph had become a legend by the time she was 20 years old.[1]

It's always a thrill to watch an inspired performance in almost any field, but Wilma's feat that day was almost beyond human comprehension. Why? "Well, that's the rest of the story, " as radio commentator Paul Harvey would say.

Wilma had hit the ground running for her life. Born prematurely, she nearly died twice from double pneumonia, and once from scarlet fever. When she was a small child in the pre-Salk era, polio badly crippled her left leg and twisted her foot inward. The best medical opinions of her day were that she'd always wear a metal brace, that she would never walk without "assistance," and that running would always be something she could only watch other children do.

But the medical opinions could not have taken into account the awesome power of the champion's heart which beat within the little girl.

E L I Z A B E T H   J E F F R I E S

The Awesome Power of Believing in Yourself

"I'm going to travel out of this small town and make my place in the world," Wilma promised herself when she was six years old. It was a huge promise for a little black girl from a large family in Tennessee during the early 1950's to make — even to herself. The farthest she had ever traveled was the 45 mile bus ride to a large hospital in Nashville, but she'd spent so much time there it was like her second home.

She would often sit for hours at night in her hospital room and dream of living in the large white house across the street. She'd see mental images of herself as a successful woman, of having happy children, and of walking and running with them.

Yet the braces she wore served as an ever-present and painful reminder of just how far away that dream was. "When can I take the braces off?" she'd ask he doctor two or three times on each visit, during the next six years. "We'll see," was about all he'd ever commit.

By the time she was 11, she began to believe she'd someday take those braces off and go out to play with the other children. She'd tell her mother about her dreams of taking the braces off, of walking, and of becoming somebody important. "Honey, the most important thing in life is for you to believe it and keep on trying," her mother would encourage her.

On one visit, the doctor suggested "a little exercise" might help her leg. She quickly formed her own definition for "a little." Although it was strictly forbidden, she began to take off her braces and stumble across the room every time both her parents left the house. A brother or sister would always stand as a "watcher."

"Doctor, I have something to show you," she halt-ingly said during a check-up. Fearing the wrath to come, she quietly took the braces off and walked across his office to him. Her mother's eyes nearly popped out.

"How long have you been doing that?" the doctor asked, trying to mask his surprise.

"For the past year," she confessed, carefully avoiding her mother's eyes. "I...sometimes...take the braces off and walk around the house," she admitted.

"Well, since you've been honest with me," said the doctor, "I'll let you start taking them off occasionally and walk around the house."

Wilma never put those braces on again!

It would be a great tribute to the indomitable human spirit if the story ended there. But that was only the beginning for the little girl who dared to believe in herself.

By the time she entered high school she'd become a basketball player and with much effort, she became the second-best player on her team.

Eventually, she mustered up the courage to tell her coach about a dream she'd begun nourishing. "If you will give me 10 minutes of your time every day, and only 10 minutes, I'll give you in return a world-class athlete," she blurted out.

The crusty old coach broke into almost uncontrol-lable laughter, but finally agreed. He was very de-manding, but she got by with some help from her friends, and actually began improving dramatically.

There was no way she could have known that the referee who called every high school game she played was Ed Temple, who coached the Tigerbelles of Ten-nessee State University (Nashville). Under his guid-ance, the Tigerbelles had developed into the fastest women's track team in America and one of the fastest in the world.

E L I Z A B E T H   J E F F R I E S

Coach Temple asked for volunteers to train for the track team, and Wilma jumped at the chance. On her second race, she discovered she could beat every girl in her school. Before long, she was outrunning every high school girl in the State of Tennessee. At 14, she joined the Tigerbelles and began serious training.

She made the U.S. Olympic team in 1956, but was eliminated in the semifinals of the 200-meter dash at the Olympics in Melbourne, Australia. She was heartbroken, and vowed she'd never again settle for anything less than a gold medal. At 16, and still in high school, she promised herself she'd win the gold medal in the 1960 Olympics.

****

They say it's not the first mile of a long journey that gets you, because you're excited about getting there. It's the dull and grueling miles in between when nothing but hope can keep you going.

When Wilma started college, there were no athletic scholarships for women, so she had to support herself by working. In addition, she began carrying a full academic load and keeping up with the rigorous team training schedule. What's more, she was required to maintain a "B" average to stay on the team.

But that didn't stop Wilma. When her rigorous schedule caused her to start falling behind the other girls, she began crawling out her dorm window and down the fire escape after "bed check" each night for several hours of training. She maintained that torturous schedule for nearly three years.

She'd made promises to herself, and whatever it took she would keep them.

"Vilma! Vilma! Vilma!" chanted the crowd in Rome.

But what became a deafening roar in Rome had begun

as a tiny ray of hope in the heart of a crippled girl in Tennessee — many years and millions of painful steps before.

The media quickly spread the legend of Wilma Rudolph around the globe. She did indeed, make her place in the world.

Later, what she enjoyed most was leading classes and seminars for athletes. Through her Wilma Rudolph Foundation in Indianapolis, financial support is given to struggling young people with big dreams. Wilma fulfilled another promise she made to herself: to help others believe in themselves.

How to Boost Your Self-Confidence Through Creative Imaging

There's an ancient Hebrew proverb which says, "As he thinketh in his heart, so is he."[2]

Earl Nightingale said the same thing in more up-to-date language: "A person becomes what he thinks about all day." After more than 2500 years of scientific exploration, the fact still holds true — our attitudes shape our actions, and our actions shape our lives. All too often we let the world around us determine what we think about most of the time.

But you can boost your self-confidence by learning how to use creative imaging.

The typical human brain weighs about three and a quarter pounds, yet it has hundreds of times more storage capacity than the largest computer ever built. An average person's brain can store over two quintillion bits of information — that's a two, followed by 18 zeroes. With the national debt being what it is, I hope Congress never discovers that figure!

Research scientists have discovered that even the most brilliant human beings - like the Einsteins and

Edisons — only use less than 10 percent of their mental powers.

But why? Why do most of us sit here with this massive source of creative energy right between our ears, and use only a small fraction of its power?

The biggest reason is that about 90 percent of our mental power is in that vast, untapped reservoir we call the subconscious mind. All of us can relate to and identify our conscious mind. We think, and we act.

Unfortunately, most of us in western civilization don't have much feeling for our subconscious minds. When we hear someone mention the subconscious, we immediately start thinking about psychiatrists, and people who do crazy things.

Yet our subconscious minds play a very active role in our lives every day. They record input from all our senses and constantly assimilate them with all our previous input. All of our actions are affected by our subconscious minds and what they believe. In fact, if we do something enough times, it becomes a habit to us, and we don't even have to consciously think about doing it.

You don't have to be a psychiatrist (or need a psychiatrist) to learn to tap into the tremendous resource of your subconscious. Wilma Rudolph, even when she was a tiny girl unlocked her hidden potential by using her subconscious mind, although it's doubtful she ever thought about it.

The simplest way to tap into our subconscious is by using our imagination. It's that place in our brains where we daydream — where we are most creative.

In our action-oriented society, we don't have much use for daydreams. For example, how many times have you heard someone say, "Don't let your imagination run away with you!" or "Don't waste your life daydreaming... You've got to make a living!"

E L I Z A B E T H   J E F F R I E S

What we often overlook is that we all think in mental images — in pictures. That's true even when we're thinking about numbers. If you read the numbers 1-2-3-, what does your mind do? It forms a mental picture of the numerals we've all come to recognize as the numbers one, two, and three. Try it! You can play with that later. It's fun to think about when you first discover it.

I said you could boost your self-confidence through creative imaging. But what is creative imaging? It's simply choosing what you see with your inner eyes. It's tuning out all the external sensory input, and tuning in to your own subconscious mind.

Actually, many research scientists believe that the biggest difference between most of us and Albert Einstein is that he was a master of creative imaging. Instead of allowing the world around him to dictate what he would think about, and define the way he would think about it, he consciously chose to think in his own images. In other words, he chose his own mental pictures.

One reason we get so many wrong answers is that we ask the wrong questions.

One reason we get so many wrong answers is that we ask the wrong questions. For example, on a national level, what's the first thing we think about when we think in terms of health care? Most of us begin immediately thinking about hospitals, doctors, and medicine. But many of America's foremost medical authorities are beginning to suggest we reframe the question and ask, "Why do people get sick?" Instead of always asking "How can people get well?"

Creative imaging not only enables us to ask the right questions; it enables us to concentrate all our creative energies in the right direction. Psychiatrist Carl Jung said, "The imagination is a concentrated extract of all the forces of life." Tapping into your imagination through creative images is like having a television camera focused in on your deepest inner resources.

So when you choose the images to feed into your mind, and allow your mind to feed back to you its wealth of insight, you've begun the process of high level communication — you've begun to communicate effectively with your own mind.

Interestingly, the better you become at communicating with your own mind, the better you'll become at communicating with other people.

Okay, if creative imaging can help you to tap into more of the tremendous power of your subconscious mind, how can you do it? It's simple enough that anyone can do it.

Learn how to relax. Your subconscious mind is most open to suggestion when you are completely relaxed. Now most of us think we know how to relax. For example, we call watching television relaxation. Some of us can even fall asleep watching a dull show. That's not at all what I mean by relaxing; that's turning your mind over to an electronic box. Usually it's a form of escape.

Really relaxing is turning out all external sensory input, and turning in to your own inner thoughts. It's getting still. It's slowing everything down to a point that your conscious mind can connect with your subconscious mind.

One good way to do it is to sit in a straight chair, with both feet flat on the floor, and with your hands resting comfortably in your lap. Then slowly concentrate on relaxing every part of your body.

Start creating mental pictures of yourself as a confident, capable person, doing whatever you want to accomplish. The more vividly you see the picture in your mind, the more effective it will be. It's the technique America's athletes use during the Olympic games. They take a few seconds before they start each event, and actually "see themselves through" their performance. They form a mental picture of themselves performing at their very best; then go out and do exactly what they've imagined themselves doing. Many of the top performers attribute much of their success to using this simple technique.

You can apply the same technique to any task you need to perform, or to every area of your life.

For example, if you're a salesperson, picture yourself going confidently through your presentation and closing the sale. Or if you're starting a new job, picture yourself confidently going through your first day and doing everything well.

Practice, practice, practice! At first it may feel a little awkward to you, but the more you do it the easier it will become. Eventually, you will be able to do it in a few seconds and without having to sit down each time.

In fact, if we do something enough times, it becomes a habit to us, and we don't even have to consciously think about doing it.

*****

Creative imaging is simply using your imagination to daydream about yourself in a positive way. It's a way of actually reprogramming your subconscious mind to think positively about yourself and your abilities.

By actively feeding positive mental images into your subconscious mind, you can reprogram it to see yourself as a confident and capable person — you can really see yourself a winner.

E L I Z A B E T H   J E F F R I E S

Master of the Art of Self-Talk

Words can sting like scorpions, and they can have a devastating effect upon our self-confidence.

For example, have you ever noticed how people are always trying to pin labels on you? They're always trying to lump you into their neat little boxes. A child who grows up being told how "stupid" he or she is will usually reach adulthood feeling that way. A person who's constantly characterized as a failure will begin acting like a failure. The fact is that we pay attention to what people say about us.

But if what others say about us has an impact upon us, it is small when compared with the effect of what we say to and about ourselves.

Memory experts, for instance, say the greatest hindrance to developing a good memory is constantly telling yourself, "I just don't have a good memory." All of us have a good memory, they say. It's just that some of us have untrained memories.

Some of us will bristle up very quickly when others are critical toward us. Yet we constantly criticize ourselves.

It can become a habit which is so deeply entrenched that we're not aware we're doing it.

Do you ever say things to yourself like:
- "I'm an undisciplined person."
- "I just go all to pieces when…"
- "I always seem to have to settle for second best."
- "I just can't help it!"
- "I'm just not good at…"

Negative statements like those can be devastating to your self-confidence. The problem is that your subconscious mind begins to believe them and to drive you to act as if they're really true.

Trying to overcome a negative self-image and low self-esteem, while constantly putting yourself down, is like trying to dig your way out of a hole. The more you dig, the deeper the hole gets. I like what former AT&T chief executive officer Charlie Brown said about that: "When you find yourself in a hole, quit digging!"

One of the most productive ways to begin to discover who you are is to quit telling yourself all the things you are not.

Say wonderful things to yourself. The easiest way to break the negative habit of always putting yourself down is to make a positive new habit of building yourself up.

Just as your subconscious mind believes all the terrible things you tell it about yourself, it also believes all the wonderful things you say to it.

There are two ways you can do this. First, practice reversing every negative thought about yourself the instant it comes up:

If You Feel Like Saying	Say Instead
"I'm a failure!"	"I am a capable person."
"I can't!"	"I can and I will!"
"I'm afraid!"	"I'm confident!"
"I have a problem."	"I have a challenge!"
"I have no special talents."	"I am a talented person!"
"I'm not very smart."	"I am learning!"

You'll be amazed at how your feelings about yourself will begin to change over the next few weeks. Set aside a time each day to actively feed positive thoughts about yourself into your subconscious mind.

I've found it helpful to do it during my morning prayer times because I'm more relaxed. Starting out the day with positive affirmations heads off negative thoughts before they can get started and sets an upbeat tone for the entire day.

Actually, we all talk to ourselves constantly. Even as you're reading this, you're talking to yourself: "What does she mean by that? Will it really work for me? That reminds me of something I read last week..."

One good way to do it is to record some positive statements in your own voice, and play them back while you're completely relaxed. Record them slowly enough to let each statement soak in after you've heard your own voice say it.

Here are some statements to get you started:
- I can feel my body relaxing all over.
- My breathing is slow and relaxed.
- I am at peace.
- I am a unique and wonderful person.
- I was created in the image of God.
- I'm glad I'm me, right now.
- I am loving and kind.
- I am strong and filled with vitality.
- Today is the best day of my life.

You'll soon get the hang of it and begin coming up with your own positive statements. That way you can tailor them to your specific situation and needs.

Cultivate a positive mental attitude by reading books and articles and by listening to energizing tapes. Never in history have there been so many good sources for positive input for our minds!

Your mind is like a sponge — it soaks up whatever is most readily available to it. All day long, every day, all of us are exposed to negative input from a wide variety of sources. It is not hard at all to find reasons to doubt your own abilities.

But you can counterbalance all that negative input by constantly taking in positive thoughts from every available source. You'll be amazed at how much it will help you boost your self-confidence.

To Sum It All Up

Some researchers claim that at least 95 percent of our actions are a result of our habits. If that's true, nothing could be more crucial to becoming a success in any venture of life than forming the positive habit of seeing ourselves as confident and capable persons. One very effective way to do that is to master the fine arts of creative imaging and positive self-talk.

Let me encourage you to pause for a few minutes of personal practice with each technique before you move on to the next chapter.

Application Exercise

1. Review the section on creative imaging and practice the steps it suggests.

2. Make your own positive self-talk cassette, using the suggested affirmations. Set aside a specific time to listen to it.

1.   Reference; Jacobs, Linda, *Wilma Rudolph: Run For Glory*, Copyright 1975 by ENC Press.

2.   Proverbs 23:7, *The Bible*, King James Version.

Six

Target Your Life

Objectives

1. To discover the benefits of setting goals.

2. To learn how to set goals.

3. To discover how to turn goals into realities.

"Cheshire-Puss...would you tell me please, which way I ought to go from here?" asked Alice.

"That depends a good deal on where you want to get to," said the Cat.

"I don't much care where," said Alice

"Then it doesn't matter which way you go," said the Cat.

— Lewis Carroll
Alice in Wonderland

Living Wholeheartedly

"Happiness is essentially a state of going somewhere wholeheartedly," said W.H. Sheldon.

One of the most pressing drives of human nature is the urge to always be doing something worthwhile with our lives. Most of us feel we simply must be doing something important with the energies we expend.

Yet, how often do you come to the end of a day feeling as if you haven't really accomplished anything? You've been busy all day — you might even have felt rushed most of the time — but you have not achieved anything you'd call important.

Usually, when we scurry around all day and feel we have nothing to show for it, it's because we have spent our time doing what was "urgent," not what was "important." There is a vast amount of difference.

"Urgencies" are those activities which seem so pressing at the moment, but have little significance in the long run. They're the thousands of things which surface every time we want to get a job done; the countless demands on our time at the moments we can least afford to concern ourselves with them.

As a result, we seldom make big decisions in life. We simply make a lot of little decisions along the way. By the time we get ready to make the big decision in a matter, it's already been decided by the myriads of little choices we've made.

For example, most of us would agree we need to put some money into savings. "Someday!" we tell ourselves, we're going to do it yet at the end of each month, it's all we can do to "pay our bills." What we may not realize is that those bills result from dozens of little spending decisions we make during each month.

But the "important" things in life are those which

have lasting impact. They're the choices which shape our lives and forge our relationships.

The problem is that what's important may not appear to be so big at any given moment. In fact, truly important things always seem to be minor when compared with other concerns which are pressing in upon us.

For example, many parents have told me they'd felt that working every night and most weekends was all they could do while their children were growing up. However, when they suddenly looked around and discovered their children had grown up and were gone, they realized just how insignificant their material concerns had been.

Benefits of Setting Goals

Life constantly serves up a smorgasbord of choices, opportunities, demands, and challenges. It is the way we respond to them which determines what our lives will be like.

The real winners at the game of life seem to get things sorted out and to know where they are going. They set up definite targets to aim for and expend all their energies in reaching those goals.

Nothing can help you win the game of life quite as effectively as setting and living by a carefully developed set of goals.

Nothing can help you win the game of life quite as effectively as setting and living by a carefully developed set of goals. Let's explore a few of the more outstanding benefits of targeted living.

Benefit #1: Goals Motivate You

Haven't you noticed how much easier it is to get moving on mornings when you are excited about what you're going to do that day? It seems to give meaning and direction to your activities all day.

"For as long as I can remember, whatever I was doing at the time was the most important thing in the world for me, " said Samuel Goldwyn, the famous Hollywood producer.

If all you are doing is getting out of bed to go to work because it's what you're supposed to do, no wonder you have problems getting yourself going in the mornings!

However, if you are working toward something that matters to you — a goal you really want to reach — motivation is no problem at all.

"Nothing great was ever achieved without enthusiasm," said Emerson.[1] Enthusiasm is sincerely believing something is worth your best efforts.

It is only when you give yourself completely to a set of goals you feel are worthy of your best that you can expect to approach each day with excitement and joyful expectation.

Benefit #2: Goals Enable You To Concentrate

William Tell had no difficulty concentrating on what he was doing — at least that famous day at Altdorf. The skilled archer focused all his attention on one little apple.

Compelled by the Austrian governor to shoot the apple off his small son's head, Tell was to have only one shot with his bow and arrow. If he missed, both he and his son would be put to death.

According to the legend, he split the apple precisely at its center.

Not many of us will ever have to concentrate on a goal so critical. Yet that legend serves to illustrate how a goal can become the focal point for our entire lives.

Without having clear goals, most of us will wander around aimlessly and work at whatever comes up. Thus we will find it difficult to achieve anything worthwhile for ourselves and those we love.

A goal which really matters to us enables us to focus all attention on a single target and to give it our best shot. Concentrated energy becomes power which is useful in getting what we want out of life.

Benefit #3: Goals Help You Invest Your Resources Wisely

Each of us awakens every day with a limited amount of time, energy, money, and many other valuable resources. We cannot possibly be all the places we'd like to be (or need to be), or do all the things we'd like to do — in a day or in a lifetime.

Goals enable you to choose precisely how you will invest your resources. They help you rank your priorities so you will be concentrating on what's really important to you and not on what only appears urgent.

When urgencies demand your attention, you will have a strong motivation to either handle them as quickly as possible or push them aside entirely.

Benefit #4: Goals Help You Keep Life In Perspective

With so much to do, and with so many tasks we'd rather not do, life can get to be pretty dull at times. We can get bogged down in trivialities. Goals help you keep life in perspective and see the reasons for everything you do.

One good example of how it helps is in the way you
handle paperwork. Since most creative and energetic
people hate doing paperwork, they keep wasting time
by shuffling the same papers around day after day. As
you have probably noticed, the volume of paperwork
will always expand to use up whatever time you allot
to it. But if you discover that some paperwork is
necessary in order for you to reach a goal that's important to you, your whole attitude toward it will change
from "doing paperwork" to "getting the job done."
You will attack it enthusiastically and do it as quickly
as possible so you can move on toward achieving your
goals.

Benefit #5: Goals help You Reach Your Full Potential

One reason so many people hate their jobs (and their
entire lives) is that they are operating far below their
potential most of the time. They spend endless hours
doing tasks which offer no challenge, require no enthusiasm and have no future.

If you really enjoy being a secretary, or a mechanic,
or a construction worker, there's nothing wrong with
that. All those are good, solid and exciting jobs for
people who like them. The rub comes when you are a
secretary and would rather be the boss; when you are a
mechanic and would rather own the garage; when you
are a construction worker who'd rather be an engineer.

Let's fact it. Most people never even come close to
reaching their full potential as creative and capable
performers. Goals give you something to keep reaching
for; a way to keep stretching your horizons. You may
never reach your full potential, but you'll come a lot
closer if you live by goals.

Benefit #6: Goals Help You Communicate What You Want From Others

Most of us would be amazed at how willing other people would be to help us get what we want out of life, if they could only figure out what it is. Unfortunately, many of us can't give even our closest loved ones a clue as to what we want from them, because we don't know what we want.

Goals help you avoid that trap. When you know clearly where you're going and how to get there, you can share that with other people so they can help you get there.

When you know where you're going, you can communicate that to others. Most people will appreciate the clear signals from you and will be surprisingly supportive.

Benefit #7: Goals Give You a Standard For Measuring Success

Most people live under the delusion that all it takes to become successful in life is to work hard, so they work hard all their lives. Unfortunately, some of the poorest and least successful people in the world are very hard workers.

A few learn that good things don't just happen — you have to make them happen. They don't wait for some wind of fate to blow them into some rich and benevolent port. They take charge and set about to build the kind of life they want.

It is far too easy to equate motion with progress, action with achievement, and fatigue with having accomplished something worth while.

Goals give you a definite standard against which to measure your effectiveness. If your goal is to reduce your debt structure by a certain amount by a certain date, you can tell instantly whether or not you've succeeded when the appointed date arrives. If you haven't reached your goal, you can determine why and plug up the holes your money keeps falling into.

How To Set Goals

Every worthwhile human achievement began as a dream in the heart of some individual or group of people.

At first, it might have been nothing more than a feeling of discontent with the way things were, or a vague desire for something better than they had at the moment. However, had it remained so poorly defined, nothing would ever have happened to bring about a change.

Perhaps that's where you are right now. You don't like your life the way it is and you have a desire for something better. Maybe you can't pin down precisely what you don't like, and you have only a general idea as to how you'd like for it to change. How can you change all that? How can you set goals which will enable you to reach more of your potential and enjoy your life more fully? It's a big and important task, but one you'll find well worth all the effort you put into it.

Here are some tips to help you set goals.

Tip #1: Identify Your Purpose In Life

Imagine for a moment that you have been sent by the President of the United States to a foreign country to deliver a crucial message. A limousine whisks you from the airport to the foreign capital, where all that nation's leaders are assembled to hear what you have to say.

"Why are you here?" asks the nation's leader.

"Uhhh! I don't know!" you stammer, after a long pause.

Unrealistic, you say? It's precisely the way many people answer when life asks, "Why are you here?" They haven't the vaguest idea as to who they are and what they are on this earth to do. Then they wonder why nothing they do ever seems to satisfy them.

> *You can never really set worthwhile goals for yourself until you come to grips with your underlying purpose in life.*

You can never really set worthwhile goals for yourself until you come to grips with your underlying purpose in life. Until you know who you are, why you're here and where you're going, your goals will always keep slipping away from you.

In the "Application Exercise" at the end of this chapter, I'm going to give you specific tasks which can help you identify your purpose in life.

Tip #2: Get Your Values Sorted Out

"You cannot consistently perform in a manner that is inconsistent with the way you see yourself," said Zig Ziglar.[2]

Far too any people equate success with making a lot of money. To them it's the only way to keep score in the game of life. But trying to build your goals around someone else's definition of success is like trying to put a square peg into a round hole. It simply won't work.

Each of us has a definite set of values which we can only violate or ignore to our own detriment. It is only when your goals are based on your own values that you have any hope of making them become realities.

What matters to you more than anything else? One way you can get a handle on that question is to imagine that you only have six months to live. Then make a list of things you'd do during that six months. Once you've really sorted out what you'd spend the last six months of your life doing, you will have a pretty good idea as to what you want your goals for the future to be.

Another important point to remember is that your life has many dimensions and is built around many relationships. It is important to set goals for every area of your life, not just your career. I'll have much more to say about this important point in the chapter titled "Keep Your Life In Balance."

Tip #3: Focus On Benefits

"I've tried making goals and they don't work for me," several people have told me in my seminars. Then they go on to tell me how they always make New Years' resolutions, and three days later they can't even re-member what they were. When I ask them to tell me some of their goals, they list things like going on a diet or saving money.

"No wonder you can't keep goals like those!" I often respond. "They sound more like sentences passed by a judge than goals a person could really get motivated to reach!"

We human beings tend to be sneaky. Given the choice of whether to do what we "ought to do" or what we really "want to do," we will usually opt for the latter. In fact, we will often sabotage our own goals if we subconsciously don't want to do whatever it takes to reach them.

The key to making goals work for you is to make goals that matter to you — to focus on that all-important question of "What's in it for me?"

The key to making goals work for you is to make goals that matter to you.

For example, most people can't get very excited about going on a diet. However, if you realize that being slimmer can help you land a better job, get you a promotion, or make you more effective at what you do, then that gives you something to really get excited about.

It will always be easier to work toward a benefit than to give up something. So build your goals around benefits to you and keep those benefits focused clearly in mind.

Tip #4: Set Specific Goals

Goals like "I want to become a better person," or "I want to read more," don't have any teeth in them so they're easy to forget about or ignore. If you only decide to do something in general, when you get around to it, you will never do anything.

The more specific your goals are, the more likely you are to keep them and the more they will do for you.

Let's say you've decided to read more, but you want to become more specific about it. If you set a goal of reading one book each week during the coming year, you will have read 52 books within a year. That's more than the typical person reads in a decade.

Also, may I suggest you shift the tone of the goal from "I want to," or "I will try to," to "I will!" Wanting and trying to never get anything done. It's when you

make it definite that you will do something that things
begin to happen.

Tip #5: Set Realistic Goals

To be productive, goals should make you stretch but
not break. They should be high enough to provide a
challenge, but not high enough to become discourag-
ing.

If, for example, you made $25,000 last year, it's pretty
unrealistic to set a goal of making $1 million during the
next year.

Choose goals you can clearly see yourself reaching.
I've found it helpful to close my eyes and actually try
to imagine myself doing whatever is required for me to
reach a goal. If I can see myself achieving a goal, then I
know it's realistic for me. If not, I pull it down to a size
I know I can handle.

It is also very helpful to sit down and figure out
precisely what it's going to take to reach a goal. If it
takes you six to eight hours to read a book, it's only
daydreaming to set your sights on reading 500 books
during the next year. The only way you could keep a
goal like that is to let everything else in your life go.

The only way to keep your "castles in the air" from
blowing away with the clouds is to make sure you can
build a foundation under them.

Tip #6: Give All Goals A Definite Timetable

Goals only have meaning when they have definite
and realistic deadlines.

May I suggest you set three types of goals:
Set long-range goals — Decide what you want to
accomplish in every area of life during the next five to

10 years. That way you will always know where you are going.

Break those long-range goals down into interme-diate goals — Things you want to accomplish during the next year or six months. Always make sure that your intermediate goals will move you toward reaching your long-range goals.

Break your intermediate goals down into short-range goals — For the next month or the next week.

Always keep in mind that failing to reach a short-range goal will push your intermediate and long-range goals back correspondingly, unless you make up for them later. The more specific your deadlines, the easier it is to stay on schedule to reach your ultimate destination.

Tip #7: Break Your Goals Down Into Bite-Sized Tasks

Your goals only become workable when you get definite about how you're going to reach them. You can call them objectives, strategies, or tasks. The important thing is to reduce your high and lofty dreams into bite-sized chunks you can get your teeth into.

"A journey of a thousand miles begins with a single step," says the wise old oriental proverb. The most ambitious and noble goal means nothing until you have reduced it to a task you can start work on immediately and tasks you can work at every day. "Yard by yard, life is hard: but inch by inch, it's a cinch," Dr. Robert Schuller often says.

How To Turn Goals Into Realities

Pointer #1

Write Your Goals Down

Goals only become tangible when you write them
down clearly and concisely — with no loopholes. Once
they're written out, with definite deadlines assigned,
it's harder to ignore them. You can rationalize your
way around them or make excuses for not meeting
them, but you can't deny that they exist.

"The palest ink is more enduring than the strongest
memory," says another ancient oriental proverb. Some
people find it helpful to write their goals out in the
form of a legal contract with themselves, complete with
penalties for failing to meet certain deadlines and
bonuses for meeting them.

Once you've written your goals down, keep them
where you can refer to them often. It's even better if
you can memorize them and repeat them to yourself
each day.

Pointer #2

Keep Your Goals In Sight — Visualize Yourself Reaching Them

Florence Chadwick was the first woman to ever swim
the English Channel. What most people don't realize is
that her success came on her second attempt.

When she set out from the coast of France to make
her historic swim in 1952, she was full of hope and
courage. The lone swimmer was surrounded by boats
filled with newsmen, well-wishers, and some skeptics.
For years she had trained vigorously to build her
stamina and disciplined her body to keep going long
after everything within her cried out to her to quit.

A heavy fog settled in and the waters became increasingly cold and choppy as she neared the coast of England.

"Come on, Florence, you can make it!" urged her mother as she handed some food to her. "It's only a few more miles! You're ahead of schedule!"

But Florence was beaten by the tortuous elements of nature that day. Finally exhausted, she asked to be pulled aboard a boat. She was heartbroken, especially when she discovered how close she'd come to her goal.

"I'm not making excuses," she later told reporters, "but I think I could have made it if I could have only seen my goals."

But Florence was not a person to be easily beaten. She was determined to try again. This time, however she added a new dimension to her daily training. She studied the shoreline of England where she expected to land, and memorized every feature of that famous seacoast. Each day as she swam, she would replay that mental image of her goal.

She again entered the waters and set out for the coast of England. Along the way, she encountered all the fog, all the turbulence, and all the cold water she'd met before: but something was different. She swam with greater vigor and determination; even the skeptics noticed her new confidence.

She succeeded and set a record which will stand forever — she became the first woman in history to swim the English Channel.

Why? She later said that it was because she was able to keep her goal clearly focused in her mind, even when she couldn't see it with her eyes.

I hope you get the point: your goals are only as secure as the vividness with which they are implanted into your mind. Visualize and no matter what arises, you will be able to keep your sense of direction.

E L I Z A B E T H   J E F F R I E S

Pointer #3

Always Take The First Step

Long-range goals can seem miles away but, if you have carefully broken them down into bite-sized tasks, you need only to keep taking the next visible step to ultimately reach them.

For example, getting a graduate degree might seem like an impossible goal to you now — especially if you are middle-aged or older. But you don't have to tackle getting a degree. All you have to do is set the wheels in motion; then do each assignment as it comes up. If you'll keep doing those assignments and passing those tests, you'll get your degree.

"Grandpa, what are you doing?" a little girl asked.

"I'm whittlin' an elephant," the old man answered.

"Oh! I could never do that.... It's too hard!" the little girl said wistfully.

"Sure you could!" grinned the wise old carver. "All you do is take a block of wood and whittle away everything that doesn't look like an elephant!"

Reaching your goals really are about that simple. It may not always be easy, but it's as simple as taking each step as it comes up.

Pointer #4

Review Your Goals Often and Check Your Progress

Monitoring your progress is a major part of living by goals. It is a good idea to build in a definite schedule or review so you can keep tabs on how well you're doing.

Each time you check your progress and see that you are on or ahead of schedule, it will give you a boost and encourage you to concentrate more completely on the priorities you have set. You can celebrate your victories and actually feel your self-confidence growing.

If you find you are running behind your schedules, you can make whatever adjustments you need to get back on track.

Pointer #5

Keep Making New Goals

You will probably be surprised at how much more effective your life becomes when you start by setting your own goals and living by them.

You might find you reach many goals long before the deadlines you had set. The temptation then is to sit back and rest on your laurels. But that's a way of settling back into the old rut of wandering around aimlessly.

To guard against that, make it a practice to constantly set new goals. Each time you find yourself nearing a goal, start searching for new territory to conquer.

Even if you don't make your goals, you'll be miles ahead because you tried. If you failed because you didn't try hard enough, start over and double your efforts. If you failed because your goals were too high to begin with, be grateful for what you did accomplish and keep working at them.

There is always an outside possibility that you'll miss your goals because you encounter some tragedy or circumstance beyond your control. If so, don't give in to self-pity. Set a new goal, and get going.

What we're talking about is not simply a matter of getting things done. We're talking about a lifestyle; a way of thinking and acting; a system for building a life.

To Sum It All Up

If you feel your life is not counting for all it could, let me urge you to take charge by setting goals for yourself. Then stay in charge by making those goals become realities.

"Apathy can only be overcome by enthusiasm, and enthusiasm can only be aroused by two things; first, an ideal which takes the imagination by storm, and second, a definite intelligible plan for carrying that plan into practice," said historian Arnold Toynbee. Why not do it now? Why not take advantage of the following "Application Exercise" to set new goals for your life? You'll be glad you did!

Application Exercise
Targeting Your Life

Part 1. Connecting With Purpose

A. Write a few thoughts telling who you are as a person. However, this time don't use any of the traditional things you would use in a resume such as: your name; age; where you live or work; educational background; biographical information; marital status; etc. Complete the statement: I am.....

B. To help you focus the question "What am I doing here?" write a brief epitaph for yourself. Reduce to a few words what you would like for people to say about you after you have departed this life:

C. Now, in one short sentence (15 words or less), write out what you feel is the purpose of your life.

E L I Z A B E T H   J E F F R I E S

Part 2. Setting Goals For Yourself

Set at least two goals for each of the major areas of
your life listed below. Remember to make them specific
and give each a deadline.

Career Goals   **Deadline Dates**

Personal Goals   **Deadline Dates**

Goals For Family Relationships   **Deadline Dates**

Goals For Friendships   **Deadline Dates**

Spiritual Goals   **Deadline Dates**

1.   Emerson, Ralph Waldo, Essays, reference The Oxford Dictionary of Quotations,
     second Edition, copyright 1955 by The Oxford University Press, London, page
     200.

2.   Ziglar, Zig, See You At The Top, copyright 1975 by Zig Ziglar, published by
     Pelican Publishing Company, Gretna, La., page 48.

S E C T I O N I I

Balance Your Life

Objectives:

1. To discover how stress occurs in your life.

2. To understand how stress affects you.

3. To learn self-management techniques for balancing your life which can help you handle stress more effectively.

Stress can and does affect every aspect of life. Though it is necessary and unavoidable, too much of it produces staggering changes in intellectual and emotional attitudes as well as in health.

— Hans Selye, M.D.

Seven

Pinpointing Stress in Your Own Life

Objectives

1. To discover how stress occurs in your life.

2. To discover 10 common sources of stress.

3. To pinpoint the stressors which affect you most often.

Fight for your highest attainable aim; but never put up resistance in vain.

— Hans Selye, M.D.

So, Who's Got Stress?

As recently as 10 years ago, most of the information available on stress centered around three myths:

1. That only "hard chargers," top executives and "high-strung" people suffer from stress-related problems.

2. That the primary sources of stress are the major changes and crises of life, or "life events."

3. That all stress is bad for you and that you can and need to eliminate it from your life.

The idea was that stress was the deadly enemy which preyed upon the emotionally weak and those who threw themselves totally into their goals, careers, and interests.

All this helped to create a false security for many who were high-risk candidates for stress problems and to add to the problems of people who were already suffering from the harmful effects of stress.

However, more recent and much more extensive research has uncovered some rather startling new information and approaches.

Some of the more dramatic and helpful findings are:

1. People who know what they want out of life and go after it usually suffer less from the effects of stress than those who take life in a more "laid back" fashion.

2. The day-to-day hassles of life can create more serious stress problems than the major "life events."

3. Some stress is inevitable and unavoidable, and it can actually be good for you; it can enrich your life and

increase your effectiveness. Thus, it is not surprising that the emphasis in dealing with stress today centers around managing it, rather than eliminating it.

In this chapter, we want to focus on how you experience stress. In later chapters, we'll offer some tested and proven techniques which can enable you to manage stress through keeping your whole life in balance.

Discover How Stress Occurs in Your Own Life

One important theme which runs like a thread through all the findings about stress is that the key to managing stress is knowing how it occurs in your own life, how it affects you, and how to deal with it before if deals with you. Awareness always precedes worthwhile change.

Awareness always precedes worthwhile change.

The dictionary defines stress as "strain" or "pressure," and who of us has not felt that at times?

Another closely related word is "tension," which means "being stretched tight." Extreme tension or stress is like being pulled apart. Dr. Hans Selye, perhaps the world's foremost authority on stress, defines it as "the body's response to any demand placed on it, whether that demand is shocking grief or pleasant relief."[1]

Ten Common Sources of Stress

Stress experts speak of events and conditions which create stress as "stressors." The more you understand the major stressors which affect you, the better you can cope with their impact.

Let's look at some of the major stressors we all face.

Stressor #1: A Time Of Radical Change

Professor Alvin Toffler says that "change is avalanching upon our heads and most people are grotesquely unprepared to cope with it."[2]

It's not simply that change is occurring, according to Dr. Toffler, but the "dizzying disorientation" of a constantly accelerating pace of change. The effect is a little like the unsteady feeling you get when you step off a roller coaster after a long ride in which you've been shaken, bounced around, jostled and subjected to breathtaking speeds. The solid ground beneath your feet seems to be moving.

To get an idea of just how powerful a stressor change is in your own life, it might be good to list all the major changes that have occurred in your life during the last 10 years. Any people who do this are surprised to find that virtually every activity, location and relationship in their whole lives has changed dramatically.

Stressor #2: Role Changes

We tend to draw our identity from the various roles we play in our daily lives. It is not at all unusual to open a conversation with a stranger by asking "What do you do?" The problem is that our society is under-going radical role changes in every area of human activity.

Traditional roles are increasingly giving way to make room for new relationships in the workplace. There are more women than ever in careers, and more women are moving up in the workforce. Although the upward mobility of women is long overdue, and (at least for some) is painfully slow, it produces a great deal of stress in several important ways.

- Both men and women find themselves constantly confused about what their counterparts expect from them.

- Women are plagued by doubts and anxieties about their career roles and their family relationships. Many seek greater achievement, power and wealth, then struggle with confusion over changes they produce in their relationships.

- Men are more uncertain about their own futures, their roles in the workplace and their families. Many feel trapped between the "sole provider" expectations of their loved ones and the new realities of the workplace.

You might find it very helpful to have a good long talk with significant people in your life to explore what pressures you or they are feeling as a result of role changes.

Stressor #3: Time Pressures

Most people feel greatly pressured by time these days. Its seems there is never enough time to get done everything that is expected of us, and much less to do all the things we want to do.

For all our labor and timesaving gadgets, we are the most hurried, frenzied, and pressurized society in history.

Part of it probably stems from the popular notion that "you can have it all." Perhaps you can have it all, but you won't have time to use it all.

There are some definite steps you can take to gain more control of your time, and we'll explore them fully in a later chapter. However, it's important to see time pressures as a big source of stress. You might find it very revealing to write out a complete list of times during a typical day when you feel the pressure of time most acutely.

Stressor #4: Conflicting Roles And Values

Guilt feelings often occur when we are confronted by confusing roles and conflicting values.

For example, so much has been said about the guilt feelings women have about balancing their careers with their families, it almost seems trite to mention it. Yet studies consistently show it's one of the greatest sources of guilt feelings and stress among both men and women today.

Many people, especially women, want success, but feel as if they don't deserve it. Some even suffer from guilt feelings over wanting or achieving it.

Since studies show that most of us have some feelings of guilt, it might be helpful to explore precisely what conflicting roles and values may be producing guilt in your own subconscious mind.

Stressor #5: Financial Pressures

Financial pressures create stress for both the "haves" and the "have nots." Those who have amassed some wealth feel pressures to gain more, to invest wisely, and to keep from losing what they've got. Those who have little or no money constantly struggle to make ends meet. Either concern can produce massive amounts of stress.

Therefore, the question is not whether you have money or not; it is how you relate to money that creates stress.

Unfortunately, many people seek to compensate for financial stress by going on spending sprees. That only adds to the tension they feel — either by tightening financial strictures or producing feelings of guilt, or perhaps even both.

Sometimes, it is helpful to just sit down and write out what financial pressures you feel and how you are coping with those pressures.

Stressor #6: Troublesome Relationships

Nothing creates more stress for the typical person than maintaining the significant relationships which give life its meaning. In fact, any time two unique individuals meet (or fail to meet), there is the potential for stress.

The deeper the potential for pain or pleasure in any human encounter, the greater the potential for stress.

Studies have shown that stress reactions rise in direct correlation to any conflict with a loved one, a friend, a boss, a co-worker, and often with a total stranger. The deeper the potential for pain or pleasure in any human encounter, the greater the potential for stress.

Interestingly, its not simply the presence or absence of conflict in a relationship which determines the amount of stress it produces. Many relationships which appear riddled with conflict manage to defuse stress, while others which look placid are laden with hidden stress. A better indicator of the presence of stress is found in the ways those conflicts are resolved.

For example, if people don't feel free to express their anger, or if conflicts are never really resolved, the stress level is greatly increased — even if no harsh words are ever spoken.

Nor is the number of relationships a person nurtures a good indication. Some people handle always being in a crowd quite well; others seem to thrive on working and living virtually alone. Loneliness, the feeling of being cut off from significant persons, can occur in the presence of the very people from whom we feel isolated. The quality of relationships, and the person's ability to relate to others, are much better indicators of the level of stress the relationships produce.

It might be helpful to take some time to sort through six or eight of the most significant relationships in your life and seek to discover how you feel about their current status. They just might be a constant source of stress for you!

Stressor #7: Negative Working Or Living Conditions

Who feels stress from their jobs or living conditions? All of us.

A survey of 5000 women, conducted by the National Association of Working Women[3] listed the 11 worst working conditions for stress as:
- A lot of pressure or responsibility without enough authority to make decisions.

- No ability to affect how work is done.

- Work is uninteresting, unchallenging.

- Work is repetitious and monotonous.

- Workload is too heavy.

- Requires working very fast.

- Work allows little input into decisions or policies affecting your work.

- Work requires a certain amount of production per hour or day.

- Cannot use skills, knowledge, training or experience.

- Work involves deadlines and/or strict time schedules.

- Do or decide things when mistakes are costly.

"Unhealthy working conditions are those that reduce a women's control over her "work pace," her style of working and her methods of handling demands that arise on the job," according to R. Chris Night, author of the article. "Stress illnesses happen most to those who are under the greatest pressure but have the least influence in the workplace," she concludes.

What it all means is that most of us suffer from some work-related stress, and the greater the pressure and lower the ability to change things, the greater the potential for stress. The same can be said for people who live in negative conditions at home, but have little power to change their lives.

It is not enough to merely recognize that your job or living conditions create stress. What is most helpful is to pinpoint how and why they create stress and when

that stress is greatest. It is only then that many of the
strategies for dealing with stress we will suggest later
will begin to make sense.

Stressor #8: Happy Events

What many people don't realize is that "happy
events" often produce stress, and that our bodies don't
know the difference. Excitement over a new job or
relationship, relief from getting out of a negative
situation, and good news which creates a change in
lifestyle can all create stress.

Dr. Selye calls it "eustress," and says his research
indicates the body reacts to it the same way it does to
stress.

You might find it quite enlightening to list some of
the "happy events" of your recent life and study how
they have affected your stress levels.

Stressor #9: Boredom

Of all the conditions which create stress, perhaps the
most unnecessary (though often the most destructive)
one is boredom. The term "boredom" implies a steady,
circular grinding motion — which is a pretty apt
description of life for many people. They use words
like "sameness," "dull," "uninteresting," and
"unchallenging" to describe their daily routine.

Yet the sources of boredom may not be as easy to
pinpoint as many of the other stressors listed. It's
usually easier to focus on external forces which cause
stress than those which come from within.

At the same time, there are many indications that all
of us have the power to change most of the conditions
which cause us to feel bored and blue — if we're
willing to pay the price. For example, getting rid of the

"nothing to do" feeling is often as easy as starting a new hobby, but people who're really caught up in boredom often find it very hard to do.

Of course, most of us feel bored at times because life cannot always be one big thrill. However, if you often feel bored, you might find it very helpful to focus for yourself when boredom most often occurs and how it makes you feel.

Stressor #10: Fears

It's obvious that fear can cause stress. When you are terrified, you can feel your body tensing up, your heart beating faster, and your lungs gasping for more air.

But stress from the most destructive fears may not be so obvious. A good example is worrying. It may never reach alarming proportions, nor even reach our conscious awareness. It just hangs on as a nagging inner feeling that things are not going to work out well.

What makes it even more destructive is that the sources of our worries are often very hard to pin down. A worry may be nothing more than a nebulous anxiety that seems to have no real origin. Or we may think we're worried about one thing when, in reality, we're worried about something entirely different. For example, we may think were worried about the financial pressures from the loss of a job, when what really worries us is our fear of failure.

Sometimes it helps just to list the things we are worried about and really sort through our deepest feelings about those things.

Pinpointing Your Stressors

I've listed a few of the more common sources of stress which are felt by most people. But stress is a very personal thing — one we all feel differently. The big question is what causes you to feel stressful?

Before you go on to explore how stress may be affecting you, let me suggest that you review the stressors I've listed and spend some time getting in touch with the sources of stress in your own life. The following "Application Exercise" can help you do just that.

Application Exercise
Pinpointing Your Stressors

Part 1. Pinpointing Your Stressors

Review the 10 common sources of stress and put a check mark beside the ones which you feel affect you:

1. Radical Change
2. Role Changes
3. Time Pressures
4. Conflicting Roles/Values
5. Financial Pressures

6. Troubled Relationships
7. Negative Working Conditions
8. Happy Events
9. Boredom
10. Fears

Part 2. Roles and Values

A. List the various roles you now play in your life.

    1.   4.

    2.   5.

    3.   6.

B. From the list you've made, select the ones which best fit the statements below:

    1. I earn prestige and recognition as...

    2. I am challenged by...

    3. I use my unique talents and education as...

C. List in order of preference the roles you are now receiving the most satisfaction from:

    1.

    2.

    3.

D. List by rank the roles you most dislike:

1.

2.

3.

Part 3. *Pinpointing Your Stressors*

List three ways you will apply what you have learned from this chapter:

1.

2.

3.

1. Selye, Hans, M.D. quoted in *Success Unlimited* Magazine, September 1980, pages 18 & 19.

2. Toffler, Alvin, Copyright 1970 by Alvin Toffler, published by Random House, Inc., New York, page 12.

3. Source: *Working Woman Reports*, published in Working Woman magazine, Copyright April 1984, pages 142-149.

Eight

Understanding How Stress Affects You

Objectives

1. To discover symptoms and warning signals of stress.

2. To discover how we create and intensify our own stress.

3. To pinpoint specific ways stress effects you.

We have seen the enemy and he is us!

— Walt Kelly in *Pogo*

Recognition: The First Step to Manage Stress

Stress has a way of creeping up on you and doing tremendous damage before you even become aware it's at work. It's a little like the proverbial frog sitting in a pan of water as it slowly heats up. If the temperature rises slowly enough, the frog will supposedly sit there until it boils to death — and never realize what is happening.

To help you avoid the creeping effect of stress, let me share with you some insights which have proven quite helpful to me.

In our last chapter, we focused on some of the forces which work to create stress in our lives. Now let's take a closer look at how those "stressors" work on us. In our next chapter, we'll zero in on some very effective ways to manage stress.

Recognizing Symptoms and Warning Signals of Stress

"Many... believe that nothing short of five years of intensive psychoanalysis will enable them to conquer their symptoms," says Dr. Midge Wilson.[1] "But there are, in fact, some effective stress-reducing techniques that are both easy to learn and to practice."

Number one on Dr. Wilson's list is to "increase your awareness of the warning signs, which can manifest themselves in a number of ways:

• Physical (upset stomach, dry mouth, or muscle aches and pains)

• Cognitive (loss of ability to concentrate, being forgetful or humorless)

- Emotional (being short-tempered, sarcastic, or demoralized)

- Behavioral (drinking more coffee, eating more sweets, or over sleeping).

  According to any leading authorities, stress can cause:
  - Mental depression, nervousness, and anxiety.
  - Insomnia and restlessness.
  - Fatigue and exhaustion.
  - Nausea or dizziness.
  - Tightness or pain in the chest.
  - Moodiness (anger, irritability, etc.).
  - Muscle pains in neck, back, arms, etc.
  - Loss of productivity and time from work.
  - Serious medical problems (hypertension, heart disease, ulcers, colitis, vision problems, etc.)

How We Create and Intensify Our Own Stress

Stress is not what happens to us. If it were, and if we had no control over it, to talk about it would be both useless and cruel.

Yet many people think of stress as something others or circumstances do to them. Haven't you heard someone say, "You make me nervous!" or "You make me so mad....!" or "I just can't help being upset!" Maybe you've said things like that to yourself and others.

The fact is that we create our own stress.

The fact is that we create our own stress. No, we don't always create the circumstances which give rise to the stress, but we do create the stress itself. Remember, stress is our reaction to what happens to us.

We use several recipes to cook up our own pots of stewing or boiling stress. Let's look at some of the more common ways we create stress for ourselves.

Stress Recipe #1: Unrealistic Expectations Of Ourselves

Most of us hold ideals for ourselves which would make Superman or Superwoman feel uptight most of the time. We often expect ourselves to accomplish more in less time than any human could possibly get done; we sometimes think all our problems can be solved by hard work; we often put ourselves under pressures to do or acquire things which we feel give us status or prestige.

Thus, many of us tend to take on responsibilities which should be delegated to someone else; promise things we can either not deliver, or deliver only with great emotional and/or physical strain; perpetuate unrealistic expectations of us within other people.

Then we react to the pressures we have created by getting tense, anxious and fatigued.

Stress Recipe #2: Undue Time Pressures

Somehow, some of us seem to feel time will stand still and wait for us to do all we'd like to get done each day. We cram our days full of activities, promise others we'll do time-consuming things, and avoid saying "no" to some of the most unrealistic requests and orders.

Unfortunately, time keeps moving relentlessly on. It never stops to ask if we are ready for it to advance to the next hour. As a result, our days become impossibly full and our nights get so booked up there's no time left to relax. Even when we do have time to relax, we are so concerned about the things we "should be doing" that rest eludes us.

Thus we often feel tired, pressured, drained, and guilty. If you ever create stress for yourself by putting yourself under time pressures, be sure to read the chapter on time management.

Stress Recipe #3: Self-Fulfilling Prophecies Of Doom

Some of us create stress for ourselves by predicting the worst outcomes from all our actions, circumstance or failures. We carry on a constant conversation with ourselves with such statements as: "I can't!" or "There's no way I can get it all done!" or "Boy, am I going to get it this time!"

Such self-defeating statements tend to hamper our effectiveness to such a degree that immobilizing panic sets in. When added to the recipe of unrealistic expectations, the combination can be a real killer.

Stress Recipe #4: Overreaction To Crises

How do you react when a crisis arises? You may be one of those people who sees every crisis as the one to end all crises. If so, you bring a great deal of stress on yourself.

For example, if an over-reactor misses a bus or plane, he or she may see it as the end of the world. "I'll be fired for sure!" or "How could I be so stupid?" the person may say. Sometimes, they will start rehearsing their excuses and explanations and anticipating they won't be believed.

Usually, overreaction is based on deep-seated fears and insecurities. Fears of failure, criticism, rejection, or loss often show up most vividly in situations we perceive as crises.

Thank goodness, most of our dire expectations never come to pass. Yet the stress we allow them to create for us can bring on even worse symptoms and problems.

Stress Recipe #5: Procrastination

It's easy to delay doing unpleasant or difficult tasks until the last minute, but to do so is to create a great deal of stress.

Some of us make procrastination a way of life. We routinely put things off, then rush like crazy to get them done.

Unfortunately, tasks we have put off are often made more unpleasant or difficult by the delay. By adding stress to them, we take on an unnecessary burden to add to the tasks themselves.

Stress Recipe #6: Intensifying Worries And Anxieties

Worry is like a wart — useless and unsightly. Yet many of us create a great deal of stress for ourselves by doing more than our share of it. It can become such a habit that we may worry about not having some pressing concern to worry about. "I must be overlooking something!" such a person may exclaim.

To make it even worse, anxiety feeds on itself and grows stronger. The more we worry, the more we find to be anxious about.

Stress Recipe #7: Unrealistic Expectations Of Others

Just as we tend to expect too much from ourselves, we also tend to expect too much from others. We may look to others to make us happy, to provide for our needs, and to build our self-esteem.

People who create stress for themselves may say things like: "If you loved me you'd know what I want," or "You just don't care about my happiness."

When others don't come through — as we think they should — we become angry, frustrated and stressful.

The problem is not with others; it's with our unrealistic expectations of them.

The point of all this is that it's not others who create stress for us; it's something we do to ourselves.

> *The problem is not with others; it's with our unrealistic expectations of them.*

It is never helpful to say, "You make me uptight!" Rather, saying "I make myself upset" is assuming responsibility for your own stress and setting the stage to do something about it.

How Does This Affect You?

But what does all this stress we create do to us? How does it affect us? Perhaps more to the point, what does stress do to you?

As we have seen, responses to stress are as widely diverse as the individuals who give those responses.

Earlier psychologists divided responses to stress into two categories — fight and flight. When confronted with a stress inducer, we either fight it or we run from it, they said.

More recent research indicates that there is a third response possible to stress: we can utilize it.

What experts all agree upon is that it's extremely important to understand precisely how stress affects you.

Our last "Application Exercise" was designed to help you get a handle on where your stress comes from. The following one can enable you to zero in on what stress does to you.

Application Exercise
How Stress Affects You

Part 1. Identifying Your Stress Responses

Here is a list of typical responses to stress. Put a
check mark beside the ones which you think apply
to you and list any you may have which are not on
the list:

Physical Responses   **Other Physical**
- Headaches
- Increased heart rate
- Indigestion
- Weight loss/gain
- Constipation/diarrhea
- Perspiration
- Tense muscles
- Menstrual disorders
- Dermatitis
- Hypertension

Behavioral Responses   **Other Behavioral**
- Aggression
- Restlessness
- Sleep problems
- Eating problems
- Interpersonal problems
- Hyperactivity
- Difficulty with decisions
- Disorganization
- Immobility
- Procrastination

Psychological Responses   **Other Psychological**

- Anxiety
- Depression
- Loss of confidence
- Feelings of helplessness
- Hopelessness
- Anger
- Apathy
- Irritability
- Withdrawal
- Talking too much

Part 2. Focusing Ways You Create or Intensify Stress

Use the list of "Stress Recipes" below to identify specific examples of ways you create or intensify stress for yourself. You might find it helpful to review what we said about each. The more specific you are, the more it will help you get a handle on what stress does to you.

How do you experience unrealistic expectations of yourself?

1.

2.

3.

How do you set undue time pressures?
1.

2.

3.

How do you experience self-fulfilling prophecies of doom?
1.

2.

3.

1.   Wilson, Midge, assistant professor of psychology at DePaul University,
     Chicago; quotes are from an article titled "First Aid For Stress," in Success
     Unlimited magazine, Copyright Success Unlimited, Inc., Chicago.

Nine

Self Management Techniques for Balancing

Objectives

1. To understand the basic concept of balancing.

2. To learn how to balance your life.

3. To select areas of your life to be balanced.

4. To discover self-management techniques for balancing your life.

Face it. Sometimes you've got to do what others want you to do. But not always!

— Alan Larkin
How to Get Control of Your Time and Your Life

Life's a Beauty When It's Balanced

I love to travel by car, especially through the lush,
green Kentucky countryside surrounding the city
where I live. Rolling smoothly along a wide open
interstate highway can be both exhilarating and relaxing. You get the feeling you're really going somewhere;
you love the changing scenery; you feel secure and
comfortable. However, there is one thing which can
take all the joy out of driving — a tire that is out of
balance.

A seriously unbalanced tire can violently shake the
whole vehicle, cause the steering wheel to tremble so
much you feel you're losing your grip, and do serious
damage to the car's shock absorbing system. Like most
drivers, I never notice my tires are there until something goes wrong. They support my weight and the
weight of my car, keep me on the road, give me momen-
tum, stop me when necessary, and help to smooth out
the bumps. I never give them a second thought until
one of them is not operating properly. But an unbalanced tire can drive me up the wall instead of down the
road. That's precisely the way it is with stress. When
your life is balanced you feel exhilarated, relaxed, in
control - like you're really getting somewhere. But
when your life gets out of balance you feel pressured,
tense, depressed, drained — like you're losing your
grip on life. Your whole being, much like an automo-
bile tire, is designed to operate in perfect balance.

"To varying degrees, we thrive on stress," says Dr.
Hans Selye. "In fact, stress is the spice of life," he
observes.[1] "The need might even be for more stress
rather than less," he continues. "There are people who
actually suffer from too little stress; who need more
activity in their lives, instead of sitting down and

silently meditating." Stress often comes from choosing, from coping, from striving, from struggling with challenges, and even from the good things which happen to us. Take away those things and life becomes bland, dull and uninteresting. We lose our competitive edge, our intensity, and our drive.

Understanding the Concept of Balancing

The great challenge of stress is not so much in eliminating it from your life, but in keeping it under control. "Look for balance," said Dr. Donald Tubesing, who compared stress to a violin string. "It needs enough tension to make music, but not to snap."[2]

We live in a universe which is totally balanced for harmonious operations. If the earth were a few miles closer to the sun, it would be an inferno; if it were a few miles further away, we'd all freeze. Balance begins with a design and a clearly thought-out plan. Even the lowest forms of life and the smallest particles of matter point to an organized scheme that constantly mystifies even the most cynical scientist. But balance is also a constant process of change and self-restoration. In recent years, scientists have been talking more and more about "ecology" and "ecosystems." They've discovered that the whole created order constantly moves to restore balance when something gets out of kilter.

Your Body Seeks To Balance Itself

Because of my earlier profession of nursing, I've always been fascinated by the wonders of the human body and its precision at seeking balance when any demand is placed upon it. For example, your body

temperature is always changing. It constantly fluctu-
ates to accommodate the slightest change in conditions.
Your body reflexively compensates for any injury you
might receive. If you step on a nail, your entire body
jerks to take the pressure off the injured foot, your
whole immune system (with all its billions of parts)
springs into action, and your lungs start gulping in
more oxygen to meet the increase demand. It's all so
automatic you probably won't even notice it's happening.

How Stress Balancing Works

As a human being, your life is just another part of
the universe which is meant to operate in perfect
balance. You need just so much work, so much play, so
much nutrition, so much rest, so much exercise, and
just so much of any other things. Get too much or too
little of anything, and the whole physiological and
psychological system is thrown out of balance — and
guess who pays the price. That's what stress is all
about: it's your response to something in your life
being thrown out of balance. The key to effectively
controlling stress is keeping your whole life in balance
and working to restore balance whenever it's lost. But
stress can be sneaky. Stress responses have a way of
cropping up in unexpected symptoms and confusing
displays.

To illustrate, let's look again at the car tire. If you
have to slam on your brakes suddenly and skid a long
distance, you'll likely be greatly relieved that you
avoided an accident. What you may not realize is that
you've scraped a good bit of tread off one side of the
tire; it's out of balance. As you pick up speed, you'll
begin to feel a slight bump in the car. If you ignore it,

the tire will wear unevenly. Ignore it long enough and it will begin to violently shake the whole car and become the center of attention every time you drive.

Stress responses operate in the same way. Let's say you get angry with someone again and again, but feel you'd better keep your mouth shut. So you keep pushing it down inside. You may begin to notice that you're more depressed than normal, but you keep going. Eventually, that anger may erupt into a severe headache, or inability to concentrate, or a host of other symptoms. Why? It's because your suppressed anger has thrown your life out of balance.

You have all the resources you need to cope with stress.

But the good news is that where there is balance, there is a sense of well being, and a feeling of peace and harmony with yourself and the whole world. There are fantastic benefits in every area of your life. It starts with designing a balanced plan for your entire life. As you sort through the various roles, values and relation-ships which shape your life, and seek to balance each of them against all the others, you'll find you have all the resources you need to cope with stress. Likewise, as you design a plan to balance your various psychologi-cal and spiritual needs you'll find yourself becoming more relaxed, more enthusiastic, and more vitally alive. Parts of your life which are no longer neglected with show their gratitude by helping you to rest better, enjoy life more, and be more effective at everything you do.

Right now, your life might seem like a complex puzzle that only a genius could sort through. The idea of trying to bring balance to all the many facets of our

life may seem like a hopeless task. Believe me, with a
few simple principles you can get a handle on balancing to control stress much more easily than you may
think. I'll give you four basic balancing principles.
Then we'll explore how you can apply them to your
own life.

Balancing Principle #1

Work With the Law of Action and Reaction

Do you remember the law of action and reaction from
your high school physics? It says: for every action,
there is an opposite and equal reaction. What that
implies for balancing is simply this: a pound of weight
on one side of a wheel must be counterbalanced by a
pound of weight on the opposite side of the wheel in
order for it to be balanced. Applied to stress, it means
that work must be counterbalanced by rest; pressure
must be counterbalanced by relief; demands must be
counterbalanced by fun and leisure; relationships must
be counterbalance by satisfying ego needs.

Balancing Principle #2:

Know Your Own Optimum Stress Level

Just as we all have different tastes in music, food and
clothing, we all have unique responses to stress. Learning how to balance means knowing and respecting
your own optimum stress level. What may be too
much stress for one person might be just enough to
energize another. "It is useless to tell a turtle that he
should beat a racehorse once in a while because he
owes it to his turtleness: that would just kill him," says
Dr. Selye.[3] It's only possible to keep your life in balance
when you know what your balance point is: that point

at which you feel energized, excited and relaxed — but not drained, depressed and chronically tired.

Balancing Principle #3:

Cultivate Enlightened Self-Interest

There is a vast difference in being self-centered and acting in your own best interest. To be self-centered is to always want your way, regardless of what it costs others or does to your relationships. It's meeting your needs at the expense of others — the kind of attitude which causes a mugger to kill an old man for a couple of dollars. Such an attitude will always ultimately lead to more stress, not less. But enlightened self-interest involves being egotistic in responsible ways. For example, it's recognizing that you need other people as much as you need to achieve in your career, and vice versa. Enlightened self-interest takes into account all your values and acts on the basis of what's best for you as a total person, not just a single faceted view.

Balancing Principle #4:

Learn How to Give And Receive

Someone once said you could divide all the people in the world into two categories: the givers and the takers. Many are finding that through balancing, they can be both givers and takers, and that they (and the world) are better off for it. It's hard to beat the simple formula espoused by the wisest teacher who ever lived: "Do unto others as you would have them do unto you." Learning to treat all others with dignity and respect may prove to be one of the best ways to stay emotionally healthy. Giving freely of yourself and your resources does far more to relieve stress for you than it does to make life better for others. Likewise, receiving

the love and support others offer you can do wonders
to enrich your life and help you live relaxed. Probably
more than anything else, giving and receiving comes
down to allowing enough time for other people to play
out their roles in your life.

Choosing Areas to Be Balanced

Using those four principles, you can proceed to
balance your life in a variety of ways. One tool I've
found helpful in balancing my life is what I call a
"Stress Balancing Wheel." It's simply a circle which is
divided into parts representing the various facets of life
to be balanced. To give you an idea of how it works,
I've drawn up two examples as follows:

Stress Balancing Wheel/Role-Relational Balancing

Stress Balancing Wheel/Psychological Balancing

By charting out the various dimensions of life you want to balance, you can see how each counterbalances the others. A variation of it would be to draw it up as a pie chart, with the spaces for the various areas being sized according to the percentage of your time you allocate to each. If you see you have one or two very large slices, and one or two very small slices, you can readily see that something is out of balance. In the "Application Exercise" at the end of the chapter, you'll have an opportunity to draw up your own charts and connect with what areas of your own life you feel need more balance.

Self-Management Techniques for Balancing

Balancing your life means self-control.

What it all boils down to is that balancing your life means self-control: taking charge of your own life; structuring your life around your optimum stress level; dealing with stress in ways that work well for you. Let me share with you some tested and proven techniques which can help you manage your life through balancing:

1. **Stay In touch With Yourself**   Clarify in your own mind what you want out of life and out of all your relationships. Learn how to turn out all the sensory and mental input from the world around you and stay in touch with your own desires, your inner resources, and your own values.

2. **Maintain A Positive Mental Attitude**   Approach stress with a positive and constructive outlook that

says, "I can cope with life." Learn to let the past go and don't drag excess baggage from it into the present. Live now!

3. **Cultivate A Sense Of Humor** A spoonful of sugar still helps the medicine go down. Don't take yourself so seriously; learn to laugh at your mistakes and the ridiculous situations you sometimes find yourself in.

4. **Manage Your Time** Don't let time manage you; take charge of it. Identify and eliminate your biggest time-wasting habits. Don't become a slave to time; concentrate on making time work for you.

5. **Train Yourself To Eliminate Stress Producers** If there are certain people or circumstances that always seem to cause you to tense up, avoid them. Choose carefully which battles you will fight and which you will flee from. Fight those that you can win and are worth what it costs to win them, and run like crazy from all others.

6. **Learn To Say "No" Nicely And Without Guilt** You don't always have to do everything anyone wants you to do. Learn how to be gracious but firm when you don't want to do something. And don't feel guilty about it — nobody can do everything!

7. **Work On Your Self-Esteem Every Day** Take time out to talk to yourself in positive terms every day and watch the positive results. Look for concrete ways of getting your ego needs met and take credit when it's due you.

8. **Cultivate Friends And Support Groups** Life can close in on you with a brutal fury sometimes, and

friends can help to get you through it. The best way to have friends is still to be a friend. In fact, all of us need support groups to help us keep our perspective on life and satisfy our need for herd warmth.

9. **Learn To Be Direct With People** Practice organizing your thinking so you can be direct with people about what you want. They can't read your mind, and won't know unless you tell them. Learn how to say things directly without being curt or offensive.

10. **Match Tasks To Energy Levels** All of us have certain periods when our energy level is low, and others when it is high. Learn what your peak times are and schedule activities which require the most creative input during the times you are sharpest. Be sure to schedule some fun during times when you have some energy to put into it.

11. **Understand The Real Sources Of Your Anger** When you're angry, find out the real source of that anger. It may not be what appears on the surface, so learn to examine your deepest feelings to discover why something upsets you as much as it does.

12. **Take Care Of Your Body** Learn to meet the needs of your body and mind through natural methods like: regular vigorous exercise; good nutrition; getting enough quality sleep; etc. Avoid using alcohol, drugs, and other destructive escapes which only give temporary relief and create more stress in the long haul.

13. **Take 15-Minute Mental Vacations** When you feel the pressure mounding, take a short break and

let your mind take you to some exotic vacation spot. You'll be a lot sharper when you get back.

14. **Schedule Leisure Time For Yourself** If you wait until you have time to relax and enjoy leisure, you'll never get around to it. Allot a certain amount of time out of every day to just goof off and do precisely what you want to do. You'll be amazed at how it will help you to keep your perspective.

15. **Practice Balance At Work** On the way to work, put yourself in a work frame of mind. Lay aside personal concerns and problems and concentrate totally on doing your best. Create variety in your work schedule, brighten up your work environment, and cultivate support groups among your coworkers. Learn how to deal with people in a detached but concerned way — learn how to empathize with others but not take on their problems.

16. **Practice Balance At Home**   Leave work at work and go all the way home. Don't spend family time processing through your feelings about work. Take time to unwind and connect with other family members. Spread the family's workload around and let everyone learn by sharing in it. Look for ways to spend quality time with your spouse and children.

17. **Stay In Touch With The God-power Within You** The Bible contains countless statements like, "Fear not!", "Don't be afraid!", "Don't worry about Tomorrow!", and "Peace be unto you!" The implications quite clear: God's peace is a tremendous aid

in dealing with stress. All we have to do is to stay in touch with the God-power within us to remain tranquil in the most threatening circumstances.

18. **Realize You Are Not Superhuman** Admit your mistakes and accept your shortcomings. You're not perfect; no one is. So cut yourself some slack and root out all perfectionistic tendencies and ideals. If you'll really be yourself, you'll find that more than adequate.

To Sum It All Up

Your life will only be as stress-controlled as it is balanced, and it will only be as balanced as you make it. In this chapter, I've sought to enable you:

. To understand the basic concept of balancing.

. To learn how to balance your life.

. To select areas of your life to be balanced.

. To discover self-management techniques for balancing your life.

Now it's your turn! I urge you to take a few minutes to work through the exercise on the next pages.

Application Exercise
Balancing

Part 1. Selecting Areas of Life to Be Balanced

Use the two circles below to create your own "Stress Balancing Wheels." For your convenience, I've listed the areas of life I used in the earlier examples. However, the more personal it is, the more helpful it will be. So choose your own title for your charts and change the categories if you like.

Sample Titles and Segment Labels for Charts

Stress Balancing Wheel	Stress Balancing Wheel
<u>Role/Relational Balancing</u>	<u>Psychological Balancing</u>
Physical	Self-Esteem
Career	Self-Confidence
Financial	Spiritual
Family	Mental
Social	Support Groups
Religious	Service

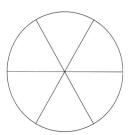 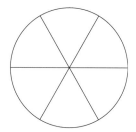

Part 2. Setting Goals for Using Self-Management Techniques

Choose three of the 18 self-management techniques and write a goal for using them:

1. Selye, Hans, M.D., quoted in *Success Unlimited* magazine, September 1980, pages 18, 19.

2. Tubesing, Donald, PhD., *Kicking Your Stress Habits*, 1983 by New American Library.

3. Selye, Hans, M.D., quoted in *Success Unlimited* magazine, September 1980, page 19.

E L I Z A B E T H   J E F F R I E S

E L I Z A B E T H   J E F F R I E S

Ten

It's About Time

Objectives

1. To become more aware of your time habits.

2. To cultivate more productive time habits.

Time goes, you say? Ah no! Alas, time stays, we go.
— Henry Austin Dobson

Balancing Time

"Time is life. It is irreversible and irreplaceable," said time expert Alan Lakein.[1] "To waste your time is to waste your life, but to master your time is to master your life and make the most of it."

I'm sure that no one needs to tell you how important it is to use your time wisely; you already know that. So I won't preach to you and try to make you feel guilty about letting time slip away. If you're like most of us, you're already fully aware that time is your most precious commodity and that you'll never have any more of it than the 168 hours a week all of us have. Rather, I'll give you some practical ideas which have worked well for me and thousands of other people. Hopefully, you'll find some insights you can use to bring more balance to your life.

Analyze Your Habits

Most of us manage our money down to the last penny. We know precisely how much we have coming in, and exactly where it's going. We draw up budgets and discipline ourselves to live by them. If we don't, we'll soon find ourselves broke and head-over-heels in debt. Unfortunately, far too many people fail to apply the same principles of management to their time — even though it's much more valuable than money.

The first step in managing your time is knowing precisely where it goes. Sure, most of us can tell you in general terms where our time goes. We know we work so many hours each day; we sleep so many hours, we spend some time eating, etc. But how do we spend our time working? Or playing? Or doing anything else? The fact is that most of us simply don't know. Let me suggest two very effective tactics for analyzing your time habits.

1. Keep A Time Log

The only sure way to find out where all your time goes is to keep a detailed time log for a definite period and carefully analyze where your time goes. Before you say, "I don't have time to mess with that" and brush the idea aside, let me tell you some of the fantastic benefits of keeping a time log:

- You'll find some holes you can plug up and save yourself a bunch of time.

- You'll probably discover there are certain times of the day, and certain days of the week, you tend to waste more time than others. That will give you a basis for improving your scheduling.

- You might discover that you are more productive at certain times of the day. Thus, you can schedule important tasks during your peak performance periods.

- When you discover how much time you spend on certain activities, you might feel it is all out of proportion to its significance. You can start looking for ways to cut the time you devote to it.

- You might also discover some very important activities that are being slighted, and you can plan to give them the time they deserve.

- You'll only have to do it periodically for it to be very helpful to you. Once you see where time goes, you can make the rational decisions necessary to assure that you manage your time rather than allowing it to manage you.

- Perhaps most important of all, it's the only way you can really know for sure where you spend your time. Until you keep a detailed time log, you can only guess where your time goes. Keeping a time log is simple and easy to do. All you have to do is write down what you do during each quarter hour or so of whatever time you're logging. Be careful not to change your regular routines so you'll get an accurate picture.

After you've kept a log for two weeks, look over you log sheets very carefully. Analyze specifically what activities get the most amounts of time and rate them as to priorities. Look for time-wasting actions and loopholes. Study the amount of time you spend with certain people and decide if it's justified. Pinpoint as precisely as you can the hours of the day when you are most productive, and those times you are least productive. In short, use the time log to study everything about the way you spend your time. I promise, if you'll take it seriously, two weeks of keeping a time log will completely change the way you relate to using your time.

2. Stage A Time-Waster Hunt

If you like, make a game out of discovering the activities which most frequently waste your time. Keep a running list of all time-wasting activities you notice during the next week. Each time you find yourself engaging in a time-waster, write down the amount of time you waste. Then add up the total times of each of your biggest time-wasters. You might find it very revealing. To get you started, here are some of the most common ways people waste time:

- Procrastination — putting things off until they end up requiring more time or until they gang up on you and take control of your schedule.

- Doing unnecessary routine work — just because you've always done it.

- Unnecessary distractions or interruptions.

- Unnecessary meetings, or meetings that last too long.

- Failure to delegate tasks to capable people.

- Lack of self-discipline in matters of time.

- Failure to set priorities.

- Unnecessary shuffling of mail and paperwork.

- Excessive socializing.

- Lack of mental control or concentration — day-dreaming at the wrong times.

- Refusing to say "no" to things that interfere with your priorities.

- Making careless mistakes that necessitate redoing work.

- Sloppy or ineffective communication.

- Failure to use management aids (like dictating machines, e-mail, and the like) to full advantage.

- Failure to insist that your co-workers carry their part of the load.[2]

The important thing is that you identify the ways
you waste time. Once you have the culprits in your
sight, don't let them get away. One by one, eliminate
them until they are all gone. You might even find it
helpful to think of them as burglars who're stealing
your most prized possessions — the invaluable moments of your life.

Cultivate More Productive Habits

Habits are like concrete: easy to manage when they're
fresh but hard to break up once they're set. Yet all of
us are creatures of habit. Most of us always put a shoe
or sock on the same foot first each morning; we either
pick up the toothpaste or the toothbrush first; etc.
Habits can be helpful or destructive to us and about all
we can do is choose which habits we will develop. Let
me offer some tips for making some productive time
management habits.

Tip #1: Make Planning A Way Of Life

The master key to all effective time management is
planning. That word scares many people, but it need
not scare you. Planning merely means "a systematic
strategy of applied consistency." In simpler terms: plan
your life and live your plan. Planning your time is
deciding in advance what you're going to do and how
you're going to do it, allocating the time needed to get
it done, and following the plan you have laid out. It
can be complex as a CPM program on a massive computer, or as simple as a few notes scribbled on a napkin.
The important thing is that you do it and that you
apply it to every area of your life.

Tip #2: Put Yourself On A Schedule

Given the choice, most people would say they'd rather live without a schedule. Unfortunately, there is no such thing as unscheduled living. You either decide your own schedule, or let other people or circumstances decide it for you. However, a schedule is nothing to be feared: it's simply a road map to guide you through the day. Of course the more complete it is, the more it can help you save time. For example, instead of merely setting aside certain hours for work, why not allocate definite time periods to accomplish specific tasks?

Tip #3: Get Your Whole Life Organized

Disorganized people are not necessary lazy. In fact, some of the hardest working people in the world work much more than they need to because they are so disorganized. They work frantically all day, conscientiously try to get everything done, and leave their offices tense because of important reports unfinished, major tasks uncompleted, and people still waiting to see them. Getting organized can help you work more easily, get more done, and make you more valuable to any organization. It keeps you from reinventing the wheel every time you need a ride; from wasting energy and time on lost motion; from feeling frustrated because you can't find things. Practice decisiveness: One thing that keeps people disorganized is that they hate to make decisions. The better you become at making decisions, the more promotable you become. Don't flounder around all day sorting through more and more facts. Gather a reasonable amount of information, study it, and then make a decision. Sure, you'll make mistakes. The only way to keep from making mistakes is to do nothing, and that's the biggest mistake of all. Besides, studies show that decisive people actually make fewer mistakes than people who struggle endlessly over every choice they must make. Don't just shuffle papers — process them: Picking up the same piece of paper again and again is a waste of time. If it's important enough to act upon, act. If it's not important enough for a decision, either file it or throw it away.

> *Excess clutter complicates every task, wastes valuable time, and leads to mistakes.*

Keep your life uncluttered. Excess clutter complicates every task, wastes valuable time, and leads to mistakes. You'll be amazed at how much your productivity will improve — how much more you'll enjoy your whole life — if you'll simply designate a place for everything and keep everything in its designated place.

Tip #4: Live By "To Do" Lists

One of the most effective devices for managing your time is also one of the simplest to use. It's the "to do" list. All you do is take a few minutes at the end of each day to write down the 5 to 10 most important things you need to get done the next day; then arrange them by priorities. The next morning, you start with your number one priority and move on through the list until you've accomplished them all. As simple as it is, it can do wonders to save your time and help you avoid frustration. "This is the most practical lesson I've ever learned," said Charles Schwab, the founder of Bethlehem Steel, to a group of budding young executives. "I had put off making a phone call for nine months," he explained, "so I decided to list it as my

number one task on the next day's agenda. That call
netted us $2 million because of a new order for steel
beams." Living by "to do" lists is the best way to
ensure that you concentrate on what's really important,
not the things that only seem urgent at the moment.

Tip #5: Concentrate On Goals, Not Activities

You can work hard all day, every day, and still not get
much done. The question is not "how hard do you
work?" but "What do you work at doing?" "Busy
work" is not productive because it doesn't go anywhere
— no matter how much time and energy it eats up.
Focus on goals, not on activities. Any time you feel
yourself rushing like mad and still coming up short on
time, review your day to see if what you've been
working on is leading you toward your goals. Wasting
motion is wasting time; wasting time is wasting your
life.

Tip #6: Develop Time Awareness

Most of us have little concept about how much time it
takes to do any given task. We almost always underestimate. Thus, we tend to not allocate enough time to
almost every task we do. Then we feel frustrated
because we can't get it all done. The mythical Murphy
was right, you know: "Anything that can go wrong will
go wrong." And he's also right in at least one of his
corollaries: "Everything takes more time than we
expect." On the other hand, we simply don't pay
attention to where they go. To combat this, each time
you find yourself wasting time, imagine an alarm going
off inside, and charge yourself an imaginary fine of a
dollar. Total it up at the end of the day to see how
much it has cost you. To see how much your time is
worth, consult the chart of the next page.

Time Value Chart

Annual Income	Value		
	1 Hour	1 Minute	1 Hour/1 Day for 1 Year
$25,000	12.81	.2134	3125
30,000	15.37	.2561	3750
35,000	7.93	.2988	4375
40,000	20.64	.3596	5036
50,000	25.62	.4268	6250

NOTE: This table is based on 244 working days of eight hours each.

By saving one hour each working day during a normal career, you can add the equivalent of six years of productivity. That's better than retiring early, with full benefits. Make no mistake about it: the more productive you become, the more valuable you are to your employer. The impact is equally dramatic in your personal life. For example, if you lie in bed 15 minutes after your alarm goes off, spend 15 minutes trying to find something to wear, wait 15 minutes for your spouse to get out of the bathroom, and spend another 15 minutes rushing to the store because you're out of milk, you've wasted an hour. It takes a little effort to become time-conscious, but it pays rich dividends.

Tip #7: Learn To Use Little Bits Of Time

What do you do when you have to wait for someone, even when you have an appointment? Or get stuck in

traffic jams? Or take long rides on airplanes?   Most
people sit and stew away precious minutes (even hours)
when that happens. That's letting circumstances and
people run your life. You can rescue that lost time by
always keeping handy some worthwhile tasks to do.
For example, it's a good time to catch up on your
chosen reading (not the outdated and irrelevant magazines usually available in waiting rooms). Or you can
use that time to do some of your routine paperwork. If
you're creative about it, you can process some of your
best ideas or write down new ones. Noel Coward,
while stranded in a traffic jam, took out a pen and
paper and wrote "I'll See You Again," one of his greatest song hits. Don't just sit there and stew. Use your
imagination to come up with productive uses for any
time you spend waiting for someone or something
beyond your control. It will not only save you time,
it'll help you keep stress under control.

*Learn to identify your prime time and guard it
with a passion.*

Tip #8: Guard Your Prime Time

Major television networks diligently guard the hours
from 8 to 11 each night. They know that's when they
will have their largest audiences and, thus, when they
can make the most money by selling commercials.
They call it "prime time." All of us have certain hours
of each day which offer us greater opportunities and
challenges than any other time during that day. It may
be because we are more alert and productive during
those hours, or because other people are most coopera-

tive with us then. Whatever the reason, learn to identify your prime time and guard it with a passion. Use it only for working towards your goals, for doing the most creative tasks, and for accomplishing what's most important. You can do the urgent things at other times.

Tip #9: Manage Interruptions

Instead of managing by objectives, many people find themselves managed by interruptions. A coworker drops in for a friendly chat; you get a dozen phone calls; you spend an hour looking for something. But interruptions can mangle your life — especially if they occur during your prime times. Here are a few suggestions for managing interruptions:

1. Manage your telephone time by a) only taking calls during certain hours, b) being direct and to the point, c) collecting all the information you need — listing what you want to cover, before you make a call, and d) hanging up as soon as you finish your business.

2. Control "live" interruptions by a) going to the other person's office whenever possible, b) removing extra chairs from your office, and c) having an understanding with coworkers that you're not to be disturbed during certain time periods.

3. Avoid having to look for things during peak periods by assembling everything you need before you being working on a project. Remember, you either manage interruptions or they will mangle your time.

Tip #10: Enjoy Your Free Time

You owe it to yourself, to your loved ones, and even to your bosses, to get plenty of rest and recreation. It's the only way you can be your best. Nowhere is self-discipline more important than in the matter of taking time to recharge your batteries. Our bodies, minds and psyches are structured so that they must have time to renew themselves. Otherwise, you will always be operating below your capacity. If you're a hard charger, it requires great self-control to set aside a regular time to relax, and then to make it stick. But, believe me, nothing matters more when it comes to managing your time.

Dale Carnegie, one of the all-time great success motivators, often used a story to illustrate this point. He told of two wood cutters who were hired to clear a large tract of land. One fellow worked at breakneck speed all day; the other stopped every hour or so to take a break. At the end of the first day, the frantic worker noticed that the other fellow's pile of wood was much large than his. "I don't understand!" he complained. "My axe has struck every time yours has today. Besides, I've worked straight through, while you sat down for about five minutes out of every hour. Yet you've cut more wood than I have!" "Did you notice," said the wise old wood cutter, "that while I was sitting, I was sharpening my axe?" That's what relaxing is all about — it's sharpening your axe.

To sum it all up

"Remember," said Thomas a Kempis, "that lost time does not return." You will never have more time than you have now; if you use it wisely, it's all the time you need. Each precious moment we have is too valuable to waste by poor and undisciplined time habits. Make it a habit to constantly cultivate more productive time habits. In seeking to balance your time and your life, I don't know of a better philosophy than the one expressed by this bit of sage advise from an unknown author:

Allow time for work; it's the price of success. Allow time for love; it's the sacrament of life. Allow time for play; it's the secret of youth. Allow time to read; it's the foundation of knowledge.

In the spirit of that advise, why not allow some time to look more closely at ways of making better use of your own time? The following "Application Exercise" can help you do just that.

Application Exercise
Balance Your Time

Part 1. Time Wasting Habits

On the next page, list several of your own time-wasting habits and a strategy for breaking each negative habit:

Habit	Strategy	Time You Will Save
1.		
2.		
3.		
4.		
5.		

Part 2. Three Actions

List at least three actions you are willing to commit to as a result of what you've learned from this chapter::

1.

2.

3.

1.   Lakein, Alan, *How To Get Control Of Your Time And Your Life*, 1983, David McKay, Inc., New York.

2.   Qubein, Nino R., *Get The Best From Yourself*, 1983, Prentice-Hall, Inc. Englewood Cliffs, N.J.

S E C T I O N III

Soul of Leadership

To the degree you give others what they want, they will give you what you want.

— Robert Conklin
How to Get People To Do Things

Eleven

Your Leading Edge

Objectives

1. To discover how to receive others into your life.

2. To discover strategies for leading others.

No man is an island, entire of itself.

— John Donne

There'll Always Be a Place for Leaders

Regardless of what kinds of new machines are invented or how dependent our world becomes on them, there will always be a demand for people who can get others to do worthwhile things.

Leadership is essentially:

1. Discovering that something is worth doing.

2. Developing a plan for getting it done, and

3. Motivating yourself and others to do it.

Sound simple? It can be a real challenge because:

• People do things for their own reasons, not yours or mine.

• Every person is as unique as we are.

• People don't always agree with us on what's worthwhile or how to do it.

• Conflicts almost always occur when great efforts are undertaken.

• Certain barriers must always be overcome before any worthwhile task can be accomplished.

In our opening chapter, we saw that getting real gets results. In this chapter, I'd like to share with you some practical ideas on how to get real with others.

First, You've Got to Understand

The soul of leadership is approaching people from the inside out. That has several important implications:

First, it means we can only lead others from a position of personal achievement. "Don't tell me how, show me!" people repeatedly say to any who would lead them. There is an old saying in the Yukon: "As goes the lead dog, so goes the team!"

The soul of leadership is approaching people from the inside out.

Second, coming *from the inside out* to lead people means you must be open and honest about who you are and what you want. People can spot a phony a mile away, and will resent being manipulated. They'd rather you be real, even if they don't like you or your plan. Besides, being yourself means you use your own personality, talents and style — and that's always the best available.

Third, it means that people want to be appreciated for who they are and recognized for what they do. "The deepest principle in human nature is the craving to be appreciated," said the philosopher William James.[1]

Fourth, most people genuinely appreciate being led to do things that make them feel good about themselves. "The mass of men lead lives of quiet desperation," said Thoreau.[2] Those who can lead such people to find meaning and purpose in life can carve out a permanent place for them in the hearts of those they would lead. So, now let's look at some practicalities of leading others.

ELIZABETH   JEFFRIES

I. Discovering You're Not Alone

Cicero, the great Roman philosopher and statesman, said the six most common mistakes human beings make are:

1. The delusion that individual advancement is made by crushing others.

2. The tendency to worry about things that cannot be changed or corrected.

3. Insisting that a thing is impossible because we cannot accomplish it.

4. Refusing to set aside trivial preferences.

5. Neglecting development and refinement of the mind and not acquiring the habit of reading and studying.

6. Attempting to compel other persons to believe and live as we do.[3]

Those observations are as true as they were when Cicero made them more than 2000 years ago.

Give People Their Proper Place In Your Life

One of the real challenges of leading others is to find the right niche for all the people in your life. There is a tendency to look to others unrealistically. We do this in several ways. First, we tend to place others above us, and to become overly dependent upon them. We end up blaming them for everything that's wrong in our lives. Second, we may place certain people beneath us. Thus, we often look down upon them with contempt and feel superior to them. We may even try to make them dependent upon us, then resent their dependence. Third, we tend to consider some people against us, and look upon them as our enemies. So we become defensive around them. Such misplacing of persons only keeps us isolated and alone.

However there is a fourth alternative: we can place people beside us. Jesus, the wisest teacher who ever lived, suggested that we relate to all other humans as our "neighbor," and that we love them as we love ourselves. The soul of leadership is learning how to balance our needs and interest against the needs and interests of the significant people in our lives.

Practice Good Human Relations

"To the degree you give others what they need, you will get what you need."[4] That wise bit of insight comes from Robert Conklin, who points out that nothing beats the golden rule for getting along well with others. Let's take a closer look at what the golden rule has to do with leadership. Basically, it means that treating other people the way we want to be treated will go a long way in motivating them to help us get what we want our of life. Here are some principles of good human relations:

Principle #1: Pay attention to other people. The greatest compliment you can pay another person is to listen to and care about what they tell you. People give more fully of themselves to leaders who genuinely seek to understand their needs, interests, and desires.

Principle #2: Give credit; don't seek it. The wise leader praises — in public — every person who gives him or her the slightest opportunity. Praising people has been proven to be 10 times as effective as criticizing them.

Principle #3: Be consistent. Moodiness has no place in the work environment — especially for leaders. Don't praise someone for an action one day because you're feeling good, then cut them down for the same action the next day because you feel badly. And don't play favorites.

Principle #4: Lose face gracefully. Be willing to admit it when you make a mistake. All of us err from time to time; to deny it is only to compound the mistake. Besides, you're in pretty good company when you goof: Henry Ford forgot to put a reverse gear in his first car; Thomas Edison once spent more than $2 million on an invention that proved useless. Also, be careful to never cause another person to lose face — even when you're right. It's better to lose face than the friendship and support of a valued coworker.

Principle #5: Learn to laugh and see the humor, even in life's toughest moments. "A good sense of humor helps to overlook the unbecoming, understand the unconventional, tolerate the unpleasant, overcome the unexpected, and outlast the unbearable," someone said. A pleasant, approachable manner can make you a hit with all whose support you need.

Principle #6: Be a good example of what you expect from others. If you want honestly, integrity, commitment and hard work from others, then give them freely yourself.

II. Mastering the Art of Leadership

What does a good leader do? More than 2500 years ago Lao Tse, the great Chinese philosopher, said:

"A leader is best

When people barely know he exists,

Not so good, when people obey and acclaim him,
Worse when they despise him.
But of a good leader, who talks little,
When his work is done, his aim fulfilled,
They will say: `We did it ourselves.'"

That's the soul of leadership — making people feel that, whatever was achieved, they did it. But how do you do that? How do you enable people to do something worthwhile?

Ten Marks Of A Good Leader

Dr. Charles A. Garfield, a leading authority on people performance, has listed 10 common traits of the highest performing leaders.[5]

1. They exhibit foresight and the ability to plan strategically. Thus, they are less consumed by short-term gain at the expense of long-term planning.

2. They decide in advance what people and other resources they will need to complete a project.

3. They refuse to become entrapped at any level of performance; they're always reaching higher.

4. Top leaders have a superior ability to take creative risks; they don't withdraw into "comfort zones."

5. They exhibit extremely high levels of self-confidence and self-worth.

6. High-achieving leaders have a significant need for responsibility and control.

7. Top leaders mentally rehearse key situations.

8. Their mission matters to them and they approach it with a great deal of enthusiasm.

9. They concentrate on solving problems rather than fixing blame.

10. High achieving leaders tend to assume ownership of their ideas and products. Dr. Garfield makes it clear that, while some people seem to naturally possess such leadership traits, others can and often do cultivate them.

Understanding What Motivates People

A big part of leading others is getting them to do the right things, in the right ways, and at the right times. But that may not be as easy as it appears on the surface. "Actually, you cannot really motivate others," says Bob Conklin.[6] "They motivate themselves. However, you can arouse and stimulate those inclinations within others that steer their thoughts and actions. So let's just say that motivation is influencing the behavior of others."

With that excellent background statement, let's look at some of the things that you can do to "motivate" others:

1. Help them feel good about themselves.

2. Stress their strengths, and help them improve their weaknesses.

3. Accept them for what they are and treat them as you'd like them to become.

4. Show interest in others, even when you disagree with their opinions and actions.

5. Show appreciation. Remember the little things like saying "Please" and "Thank you." Ask them to do things; don't order them around.

6. Give recognition. Bob Conklin says that 90 percent of what we do is done for recognition. If you don't believe recognition is important to you, ask yourself who's the first person you look for in a group picture? It's equally important to others.

7. Apologize when you realize you are wrong or have inconvenienced someone.

To Sum It All Up

To really receive others into your life means to constantly seek to enable them to grow, and to grow with them. It is not weakness to need others; you show weakness only when you fail to give others their proper place in your life. I hope you'll ponder long and hard over some of the issues raised in this chapter and seek to become the leader I know you're capable of becoming.

Application Exercise
Focus on Leading Others

Identifying Leadership Qualities and Techniques

A. Identify a person whom you'd consider a great leader:

B. List at least three qualities or traits that make her/ him a great leader in your eyes:

1.

2.

3.

1.   James, William, "Bits & Pieces"; Vol. D, No. 5, copyright MCMLXXXIII, The Economic Press, Inc., Fairfield, N.J. 07006, pg. 1.

2.   Thoreau, Henry David; *Walden, Economy, The Oxford Dictionary of Quotations, Second Edition*, Copyright 1955 by Oxford University Press, London E.C. 4, Pg. 546.

3.   Cicero, Marcus Tertullus; 106-43 B.C. Roman Consul, writer and philosopher.

4.   Conklin, Robert, *How To Get People To Do Things*, 1979, Ballentine Books/ Random House, Inc., New York.

5.   Garfield, Charles, PhD., *Peak Performance*, 1984, Tarcher/Houghton Mifflin.

6.   Conklin, Robert, *How To Get People To Do Things*, 1979, Ballentine Books/ Random House, Inc., New York.

Twelve

Mastering Effective Communication

Objectives

1. To discover three facets of effective communication.

2. To learn how to listen creatively.

3. To learn how to send verbal messages more effectively.

4. To learn how to send nonverbal messages more effectively.

The problem with communication is the illusion that it has been accomplished.

— George Bernard Shaw

Three Facets of Effective Communication

Effective communication is like a priceless diamond -
it has many facets, each glittering with exciting possibilities. Let's zero in on three of those facets which can
help you get more of whatever you want out of life:
. Receiving and understanding messages.

. Sending effective verbal messages.

. Sending and receiving nonverbal messages.

It is only when you master each of those three facets
that you can become an effective communicator. This
chapter will enable you to get a clearer understanding
of how each of the facets can work for or against you,
and offer suggestions as to how you can improve your
batting average as a communicator.

The Hazardous Pursuit

Communicating with other people is one of the most
vital activities of human beings, yet one of the most
hazardous; it's becoming a bigger challenge every day.
The problem is not that we don't talk to each other
anymore, as some have observed. Heaven knows we
over communicate, if anything. Everywhere you look
and listen, someone is trying to tell someone else
something. Rather, it's that we don't communicate
effectively. We send messages others don't receive, or
receive incorrectly; we don't pick up the meanings of
messages other send to us; we ignore the power of
nonverbal messages, both going out and coming in.

Taking On The Challenge

A major part of taking charge of your life is taking full responsibility for all your communications. That means you can never be satisfied to blame somebody else for a breakdown in communications. But when you assume all responsibility for effective communication with others, you start making, not letting, things happen in your life. Now that's a big order, especially with all the poor communicators most of us meet every day. Yet it's one of the greatest ways you and I can get more of whatever we want out of our lives.

Taking charge of your life is taking full responsibility for all your communications.

Receiving and Understanding Messages

Receiving and understanding messages is the most crucial dimension of communicating effectively. What makes that a startling statement is that most of our attention focuses on the sending of messages. Schools and textbooks teach people how to use language, how to convey meanings through words, sentences and other structures, and how to speak both publicly and privately. Yet little attention is given in education to the vital process of receiving and understanding.

I believe that creative listening could solve some of the world's greatest problems. At least, it could enable people to work together toward finding solutions. On a more personal level, it can also make a big difference. Legendary pianist Arthur Rubenstein, who spoke fluently in eight languages, one told an amusing story on himself.[1]

Some years ago, he developed a severe and stubborn
case of hoarseness, and feared the worst. Newspapers
were full of stories about smoking and cancer, so he
decided to consult one of the leading throat specialists
in the world. "I searched his face for the slightest clue
during the 30-minute examination," said Rubenstein,
"but he was expressionless. He told me to come back
the next day. I went home full of fears, and I didn't
sleep that night." The next day he went through
another long and silent examination. "Tell me," the
grand old maestro shouted. "I can stand the truth. I've
lived a full, rich life. What's wrong with me?" After a
long pause, the physician gave his expert diagnosis:
"You talk too much." What makes that story so appro-
priate to our discussion is a sign which used to hang on
the wall of Lyndon B. Johnson, when he was a junior
senator from Texas. It read: " When you ain't list'nin',
you ain't learnin'."

All Communication Is Dialog

The communications process involves more than
words. It has to do with meanings, with feelings, and
with understandings. No one can communicate with a
computer, as remarkable as they are. Only humans
beings have the capacity to grasp our meanings, to care
about out feelings and concerns, and to understand
each other. It's only when we can connect fully with
others that we can begin the process of conveying our
meanings, our feelings, and what we care about.

Fine Art Of Paying Attention

What we're really talking about is a concept as old as
the hills — paying attention. We want others to pay
attention to us. The problem is that there are so many

voices screaming for attention, it seems ours gets lost in
the shuffle; amusing radio and television commercials
cry for attention; newspapers and magazines use clever
graphics and slogans; people at home make bids for
attention; coworkers and bosses try to get your attention, etc. *The best way to get others to pay attention to
you is to pay attention of them.*

No wonder people, in an age of exploding knowledge
and greater noise, are paying less and less attention to
any of them! Keeping up with all the input from so
many sources is enough to short-circuit even the most
brilliant of minds. How do we break through all that
interference and make sure that people pay attention to
us? The best way to get others to pay attention to you
is to pay attention to them.

Don't you naturally pay attention to those people
who really pay attention to you? We humans are just
built that way. We want to be understood; to matter to
others; to know that others concern themselves with
what matters to us. And when others pay attention to
us, we reciprocate by paying attention to them.

The key to all effective communication is identification.

That's why I believe the key to all effective communication is identification. People pay attention to what
matters to them. If you want to get a grandmother's
attention, talk to her about her grandchild. Instant
attention! If you want a rabid golfer's attention, talk to
him or her about golf. Rapt attention!

Maybe you feel you don't have time for all this
business or creative listening and paying attention.
Consider how much time you lose by not paying
attention to others.

First, you lose time because you don't understand what they say, or at least what they mean. It's amazing how much confusion can be eliminated if we will just pay attention to each other.

Second, you lose time because you make more mistakes. A waiter who half-hears an order, an executive who half-hears a complaint or idea, or the parent who half-hears a child's request could all save everybody a lot of time and grief by taking time to pay attention.

Third, you lose time because you have to repeat yourself, and people still don't get your messages. If you treat a waiter or clerk like a robot, don't be surprised if they pay little attention to your requests. Identify with their concerns and you'll be amazed at how little you have to repeat your requests.

That brings us to the question of how to pay attention to others. Here are three suggestions:

1. Be An Assertive Listener

It's interesting that while most people think of themselves as good listeners, studies consistently show that the average person seldom really listens to others. Did you notice I said "listen," not "hear"? Hearing is the physical response of the ears and inner mechanism which picks up sound waves and translates them into meaningful data. We hear things like the noise of traffic, the roar of the ocean's waves, or the constant drone of a machine. But most of us have become pretty good at "tuning out" such noises.

On the other hand, listening is the positive and creative process of translating sound waves into meanings. Hearing is a passive and automatic physical response to vibrations; listening is an act of the will, and a conscious effort to pay attention. Poor communicators are assertive at talking, effective communicators are creative at listening.

2. Listen Creatively

Here are some tested and proven pointers to enable you to become a good listener:

- Open your mind and ears — be receptive to the messages the person is giving.

- Start listening from the first word. Lay aside what you're doing or preoccupied with, and give your undivided attention.

- Zero in on what is being said. Avoid trying to figure out what the person is going to say; you may miss what he or she actually says.

- Don't try to read your own meanings into what you think the person is saying. Actively assist the other person in conveying his or her meanings accurately to you.

- Never interrupt! It cuts off the flow of meaningful dialog. Besides, it's offensive and rude.

- Use questions to encourage people to talk and to clarify your understanding of what they mean.

- Make mental notes of important points. Look for connections between apparently isolated remarks.

- Control outside interruptions and distractions.

- Get your whole body involved in listening and show that you are paying attention. Look the person squarely into the eyes; use facial expressions and gesture to show you hear and understand what's being said.

- Stay cool! Don't overreact to highly charged words and tones. Hear the person out; then respond. Most people will cool down and begin to talk calmly once their anger and frustrations are vented. Remember: your goal is to be an effective communicator, not to merely "get your two cents worth in."

3. Seek To Understand

Words can be very confusing because they often have so many different meanings. For example, "Fire" can mean a consuming heat, or to let a person go, or to excite enthusiasm. Fire is what you do when you shoot a gun, or put ceramics into a kiln, or start up your car. You could probably come up with many more uses for that one little four-letter word. It's what makes communication such a hazardous activity. The same words have different meanings to different people, and in different contexts. Effective communicators learn to wade through all that confusion to seek for the meanings behind the words and actions of others. All our technology can enable us to send and receive more and more messages, but we will become robots the moment we cease to focus most of our attention upon meanings, feelings, desires and concerns.

Verbal Messages That Get Results

The main purpose of all communication is to gain a desired response. When you talk, you want action. You want people to laugh or cry with you; to care about what you want; sometimes you want them to do something. Before that can happen, they have to receive and understand your meanings. Effective communicators assume the responsibility for making sure others receive and understand their messages.

Make Sure They Hear You

My colleague, Nido Qubein, is one of the most effective speakers I've ever heard. He came to America in 1966 as a recent high school graduate, with virtually no money and unable to speak the English language. Fifteen years later, he was named president of the National Speaker's Association, an organization made up at that time of more than 2000 of the world's top professional speakers. Today, he's in great demand as a keynote speaker, an author, a management consultant, and a radio personality. He's also a very successful business leader. How could someone start from so far behind and rise to the top so quickly? He had to get a lot of people to pay attention to him and what he wanted to say. His 10-point formula is simple:

. Be natural, be yourself, be real.

. Set a conducive atmosphere.

. Always look your best.

. Establish your authority to speak on a subject.

. Organize what you want to say — don't ramble.

. Speak to needs — use words that have meaning to your audience.

. Involve your audience.

. Be enthusiastic — keep your voice lively.

. Be humorous — remember, "A spoonful of sugar helps the medicine go down."

. Use visual aids — people remember more of what they see than what they hear.[2]

It might appear that those only apply to public speaking situations. But on closer examination, you'll see they are excellent pointers for any form of communication. Let me suggest you review them for a while to see how they apply to the most difficult communication situations you face right now.

Make Sure They Understand You

The professor's wife asked for a mink coat for Christmas. "Previous extravagances preclude such an ostentatious acquisition at the present juncture," came his instant reply.

"I don't get it!" replied his less-than-refined wife.

"That's right, honey! You don't get it!" he answered.

She didn't understand his first message, but his last word was quite clear. You don't want to impress people with what you know; you want to make them understand what you mean. Here are some tips on how you can more often make them understand more of what you say:

. Use plain talk. Stay away from slang, jargon, and complicated words.

. Use words that are crystal clear and say precisely what you mean. Practice choosing just the right word for each person you talk to.

. Use active words — words that are alive with meaning.

. Use vivid images and illustrations. Word pictures are like windows — they let in light.

. Use simple sentences.

. Ask questions to keep people involved.

. Be concise, so what you do say will be easier to digest.

Make Sure They Believe You

People will only give you the response you desire when they believe what you're telling them. Here are some pointers on how you can improve your credibility:

. Say only what you're sure is true. One great advantage of talking less is that you can't be proven wrong as often.

. Test your facts and conclusions to make sure they're correct.

. Don't make a big deal out of insignificant but controversial ideas. The boy who cried wolf was right in the end, but he'd lost his credibility.

. Prove points that can be easily questioned. Raw data is usually the most convincing argument.

. Build confidence gradually. People question new ideas, especially from people they don't know.

. Don't assume people believe you — make sure.

. When you've made a mistake, admit it and clear it up. It's an even bigger mistake to try to hide or deny it.

Remember, your effectiveness in communicating is directly proportional to how much people believe what you say.

Make Sure They Care

When people care enough, they'll act the way you want them to. Persuasion is making people care about what you say. The more personal something is, the more people care about it. For example, an airline schedule is probably pretty boring to most people. But if you're planning a trip to some exotic place, that schedule can become intensely interesting. When you want people to care about your meaning, present your ideas or requests in terms that matter to them. A memo reading "Present economic conditions require that we watch all expenditures very closely" can easily be ignored. But if you say, "If we watch our money closely enough, all of us may be able to keep our jobs," you can be sure they'll care.

Make Sure They Respond

The ultimate question for all communication attempts is "Did you get the response you came after?" Whether you're selling, asking for a date, negotiating, or simply trying to inform someone, you always have a desired response. It's a good idea to test constantly, through feedback, to make sure people understand; then follow up to make sure that they have given the response you desired.

Controlling Your Nonverbal Messages

Nonverbal communication is far too big a subject to be covered adequately as a subhead in a chapter, so all I can do is tell you how important it is and point out some crucial areas to watch. You'll find some excellent books on the subject in the business or communication sections of any good library.

Scientists say we learn more than 80 percent of what we know through our eyes. That means upwards of 80 percent of what we communicate to others is through nonverbal signals.

The way you look sets the stage for whatever you say. In that critical first two or three seconds after meeting a stranger, we make up our minds how receptive we will be to anything he or she does or says. Certainly, it's a free country and you can look any way you choose. But it is also true that people have the right to tune you in or out. If you want to be heard, always look your best. You never get a second chance to make a first impression.

Good communicators are also good actors. They know that people watch their facial expressions, their body language, their gestures, and everything they do.

In fact, what you do often has a great impact on the way people interpret what you say. For example, if you smile broadly, make a feeble gesture toward a door, and say "Let's go!", somebody might rise to follow you. But if you pull off your coat, ball up your fists, and put on a snarling expression, and then say "Let's go!" you'd better be ready for action.

Those are extreme examples, but those little gestures, facial expressions, and body movements play a bigger role in communicating then many of us realize.

To Sum It All Up

Effective communication is both an art and a science. As an art, it can always be improved, lends itself to personal adaptations, and can be a great source of enrichment for every area of your life. As a science, it has certain guidelines and ground rules which must be followed. The more you study and practice it, the better you can become; the better you communicate, the more you can get of whatever you want out of life.

Application Exercise
Three Facets Of Effective Communication

Part I. Creative Listening

Review the "10 Tips On Assertive Listening," and rate yourself on a scale of one to five on each of them. If you're not satisfied with your listening skills, practice until you are the kind of listener you want to be.

Part II. Sending Messages To Get Action

Review the 10-point Formula for getting people to pay attention to you and rate yourself on a scale of one to 10 on each of them.

Part III. Setting Goals

List three goals you are willing to commit to for improving your communication skills:

1.

2.

3.

1.   Reference, "Bits and Pieces," Vol. 13, No. 7, Copyright 1980 by The Economics Press Inc., Fairfield, N.J., pg. 9.

2.   Qubein, Nido R., *Get The Best From Yourself*, Prentice Hall, pg. 140.

Epilogue
Don't Give Up, No Matter What

Your life can be all you ever dreamed it could be, and even more. But, there is only one person who can make it happen — you. I've sought to share with you some of the most valuable insights and principles which have guided me through the rough spots of my own life. They have worked for me. I hope they will be useful to you.

Perhaps the most important thing I've said in this whole book is, "You've gotta' believe." See, if you believe, really believe, in God, in yourself and other people, you'll be amazed at how many of your dreams will come true. When you believe, you love. When you love, you connect. When you connect, you truly live! I'd like to leave you with this anonymous bit of verse which have meant so much to me:

Don't Quit

When things go wrong, as they sometimes will,
When the road you're trudging seems all up hill,
When the funds are low and the debts are high,
And you want to smile, but you have to sigh,
When care is pressing you down a bit,
Rest if you must — but don't you quit.

Life is queer with its twists and turns,
As everyone of us sometimes learns,
And many a failure turns about
When he might have won had he stuck it out;
Don't give up, though the pace seems slow —
You might succeed with another blow.

Often, the goal is nearer than
It seems to a faint and faltering man,
Often, the struggler has given up
When he might have captured the victor's cup,
And he learned too late; when the night slipped
down
How close he was to the golden crown.

Success is failure turned inside out —
The silver tint of the clouds of doubt —
And you never can tell how close you are,
It may be near when it seems afar;
So stick to the fight when you're hardest hit —
It's when things seem worst that you mustn't quit.

ELIZABETH   JEFFRIES

About the Author

Elizabeth Jeffries is a recognized leader in personal and organizational leadership development. She is professional speaker, seminar leader, consultant and author, known for her high energy, inspirational message and practical approach to people and life. She draws on her years of education and experience in management and sales, packing her writings and programs with proven techniques to increase personal productivity. Her client list includes Fortune 500 companies, health care organizations and professional associations.

Elizabeth does more than teach leadership — she is a leader. She serves on several corporate Boards and has received numerous leadership awards including Woman of Achievement in Small Business Enterprise. A past director of the National Speakers Association, Elizabeth has earned its prestigious designation of CSP — Certified Speaking Professional — and has been honored with the elite lifetime award, CPAE, the Council of Peers Award for Excellence.

For information regarding speeches and seminars, Elizabeth Jeffries may be reached at P.O. Box 24475, Louisville Kentucky 40224, or at 502-339-1600.

ELIZABETH   JEFFRIES